Praise for *The Well-Timed Strategy*

"Don't miss this guide to surviving—and thriving—during topsy-turvy industry fluctuations."

—Kirkus Reports

"This book is a virtual tour de force of strategies and tactics being used by some of best 'Master Cyclist' business executives in the world. Using a wealth of real-world examples, Navarro clearly explains the dos and don'ts of timing important executive decisions to the business cycle—so much so that after reading this book, you'll view the business cycle more as a strategic partner rather than an economic adversary."

—Lakshman Achuthan, Managing Director, Economic Cycle Research Institute

"A path-breaking book full of useful war stories from the front lines. As Lance Armstrong would advise, you don't win a race in the flats—but in the mountains, by managing the ascents and descents better than your competition. Navarro shows us how the same is true for how businesses navigate the ups and downs of the business cycle."

—Stephan G. Richter, Publisher and Editor-in-Chief, theGlobalist.com

"Peter Navarro is that rare academic whose expertise spans both strategic management and technical economics—and writes like a dream. Here, he clearly explains how an understanding of the economics of business cycles gives managers a huge advantage in strategic planning while offering many compelling examples of how companies have succeeded or failed according to their reading of the impact of macroeconomics on their industries."

—Peter Passell, Senior Fellow at the Milken Institute and Editor of the *Milken Institute Review*

"Peter Navarro has written a remarkable, path-breaking book about strategic management of the business cycle that is destined to be a classic in both corporate boardrooms and business schools. Using a rich array of real world examples, he shows why corporate leaders must always be proactive, often counter-cyclical, and ever nimble."

—Bernard Baumohl, Executive Director of the Economic Outlook Group and Author of *The Secrets of Economic Indicators*

The Well-Timed Strategy

Ideas. Action. Impact.
Wharton School Publishing

In the face of accelerating turbulence and change, business leaders and policy makers need new ways of thinking to sustain performance and growth.

Wharton School Publishing offers a trusted source for stimulating ideas from thought leaders who provide new mental models to address changes in strategy, management, and finance. We seek out authors from diverse disciplines with a profound understanding of change and its implications. We offer books and tools that help executives respond to the challenge of change.

Every book and management tool we publish meets quality standards set by The Wharton School of the University of Pennsylvania. Each title is reviewed by the Wharton School Publishing Editorial Board before being given Wharton's seal of approval. This ensures that Wharton publications are timely, relevant, important, conceptually sound or empirically based, and implementable.

To fit our readers' learning preferences, Wharton publications are available in multiple formats, including books, audio, and electronic.

To find out more about our books and management tools, visit us at whartonsp.com and Wharton's executive education site, exceed.wharton.upenn.edu.

The Well-Timed Strategy

Managing the Business Cycle for Competitive Advantage

■■ Peter Navarro ■■

Ideas. Action. Impact.
**Wharton School
Publishing**

Library of Congress Cataloging-in-Publication Data

Navarro, Peter.
  A well-timed strategy : managing the business cycle for competitive advantage / Peter Navarro.
     p. cm.
  Includes bibliographical references and index.
  ISBN 0-13-149420-1
  1. Strategic planning. 2. Competition. 3. Business cycles. I. Title.
  HD30.28.N3889 2006
  658.4'012—dc22
                                        2005020851

Publisher: Tim Moore
Wharton Editor: Yoram (Jerry) Wind
Executive Editor: Jim Boyd
Editorial Assistant: Susan Abraham
Development Editor: Russ Hall
Marketing Manager: John Pierce
International Marketing Manager: Tim Galligan
Cover Designer: Alan Clements
Graphic Designer: Laura Coyle
Managing Editor: Gina Kanouse
Senior Project Editor: Kristy Hart
Copy Editor: Keith Cline
Indexer: Lisa Stumpf
Senior Compositor: Gloria Schurick
Manufacturing Buyer: Dan Uhrig

Ideas. Action. Impact.
Wharton School Publishing

© 2006 by Pearson Education, Inc.
Publishing as Wharton School Publishing
Upper Saddle River, New Jersey 07458

Wharton School Publishing offers excellent discounts on this book when ordered in quantity for bulk purchases or special sales. For more information, please contact U.S. Corporate and Government Sales, 1-800-382-3419, corpsales@pearsontechgroup.com. For sales outside the U.S., please contact International Sales at international@pearsoned.com.

Printed in the United States of America

First Printing, January 2006

ISBN 0-13-149420-1

Pearson Education LTD.
Pearson Education Australia PTY, Limited.
Pearson Education Singapore, Pte. Ltd.
Pearson Education North Asia, Ltd.
Pearson Education Canada, Ltd.
Pearson Educatión de Mexico, S.A. de C.V.
Pearson Education—Japan
Pearson Education Malaysia, Pte. Ltd.

Receive Special Benefits by Registering This Book

Register this book today and receive exclusive benefits that you can't obtain anywhere else, including

- Updates to the Master Cyclist Research Project, access to a weekly newsletter from the author, and audio commentary.

- A coupon to be used on your next purchase

To register this book, use the following special code when you visit your My Account page on Whartonsp.com:

Special Code: **etertegy4201**

Note that the benefits for registering may vary from book to book. To see the benefits associated with a particular book, you must be a member and submit the book's ISBN (the ISBN is the number on the back of this book that starts with 0-13-) on the registration page.

113240

Ideas. Action. Impact.
**Wharton School
Publishing**

Bernard Baumohl
THE SECRETS OF ECONOMIC INDICATORS
Hidden Clues to Future Economic Trends and Investment Opportunities

Randall Billingsley
UNDERSTANDING ARBITRAGE
An Intuitive Approach to Investment Analysis

Sayan Chatterjee
FAILSAFE STRATEGIES
Profit and Grow from Risks That Others Avoid

Tony Davila, Marc Epstein, and Robert Shelton
MAKING INNOVATION WORK
How to Manage It, Measure It, and Profit from It

Sunil Gupta, Donald R. Lehmann
MANAGING CUSTOMERS AS INVESTMENTS
The Strategic Value of Customers in the Long Run

Stuart L. Hart
CAPITALISM AT THE CROSSROADS
The Unlimited Business Opportunities in Solving the World's Most Difficult Problems

Lawrence G. Hrebiniak
MAKING STRATEGY WORK
Leading Effective Execution and Change

Jon M. Huntsman
WINNERS NEVER CHEAT
Everyday Values We Learned as Children (But May Have Forgotten)

Eamonn Kelly
POWERFUL TIMES
Rising to the Challenge of Our Uncertain World

Doug Lennick, Fred Kiel
MORAL INTELLIGENCE
Enhancing Business Performance and Leadership Success

Vijay Mahajan, Kamini Banga
THE 86 PERCENT SOLUTION
How to Succeed in the Biggest Market Opportunity of the Next 50 Years

Alfred A. Marcus
BIG WINNERS AND BIG LOSERS
The 4 Secrets of Long-Term Business Success and Failure

Robert Mittelstaedt
WILL YOUR NEXT MISTAKE BE FATAL?
Avoiding the Chain of Mistakes That Can Destroy Your Organization

Peter Navarro
THE WELL-TIMED STRATEGY
Managing the Business Cycle for Competitive Advantage

This book is dedicated to:

Chris Bergonzi—who persisted on principle,

Barbara Rifkind—who believed in the big idea,

Russ Hall—who helped spot the diamonds and smooth out the rough,

John Clarke and Gary Black—who made the technology possible,

Pedro Sottile—who made it all possible, and

Lisa Munro and Cecile Richardson—who early on showed the team the way.

Master Cyclist: **Mas·ter Cy·clist** [n] (1) a champion bike racer; (2) A business executive who skillfully deploys a set of well-timed strategies and tactics to manage the business cycle for competitive advantage. **Antonym**: reactive cyclist

CONTENTS

About the Author

Peter Navarro is a business professor at the University of California-Irvine and author of the bestselling investment book *If It's Raining in Brazil, Buy Starbucks*. His unique and internationally recognized expertise lies in his "big picture" application of a highly sophisticated but easily accessible macroeconomic analysis of the business environment and financial markets.

His articles have appeared in a wide range of publications, from *Business Week*, the *Los Angeles Times*, *New York Times*, and *Wall Street Journal* to the *Harvard Business Review*, the *Sloan Management Review*, and the *Journal of Business*. Professor Navarro is a widely sought after and gifted public speaker. He has appeared frequently on Bloomberg TV and radio, CNN, CNBC, and NPR as well as on all three major network news shows.

Introduction

As inexorably as the sun rises and sets, the business cycle moves from a bright and healthy expansion and prosperous peak to a dark and often difficult recessionary trough and then back once again to prosperity. Over the course of this often dangerous economic roller coaster, the fortunes of most companies quite literally ebb and flow while at least some companies, caught totally unaware by the advent of recession, will tumble down the trapdoor of bankruptcy—often never to rise again.

Over the course of the business cycle so, too, is it that thousands of jobs are created in boom times while thousands more are again lost when things inevitably go bust. Meanwhile, millions of stock market investors—from penny-pinching pensioners to Master of the Universe mutual fund managers—will watch their portfolios exuberantly grow, then troublingly shrink and, if they are lucky or skilled enough, watch them grow once more again.

Despite the profound impact that the business cycle has on the fortunes and fate of so many businesses large and small—and the employees and investors that depend on them—*you will not find a single book that offers a comprehensive guide to strategically and tactically managing the business cycle.* This gaping gap on the managerial bookshelf is truly the "black hole" of corporate strategy—for it is arguably the case that the business cycle is one of the single most important determinants of corporate profitability and stock price performance.

Moreover, this lack of a comprehensive guide to managing the business cycle is all the more astonishing because, as I demonstrate shortly, the business cycle is not just fraught with numerous dangers. Its key expansionary and recessionary turning points also offer up a veritable cornucopia of profitable opportunities for the business cycle–sensitive corporate executive team.

The purpose of this book is to teach you how to effectively and presciently exploit these considerable opportunities—and thereby gain a powerful competitive advantage over your business rivals. I do so by illustrating a comprehensive set of well-timed strategies and tactics that you can deploy over the six major areas of "Master Cyclist" management.

These Master Cyclist management areas encompass virtually every major activity of the modern corporation. They range from the functional areas of marketing, production, supply chain management, and human resources to the all-important timing of capital expenditure programs, the equally timely execution of acquisition and divestiture strategies, and the intricate methods used not just to hedge business cycle risk but also to tactically exploit its opportunities.

Each of the well-timed strategies and tactics that this book introduces you to have all been "battle tested" and proven to lead to superior performance. Each has been developed from the extensive research of the Master Cyclist Project conducted at the Paul Merage School of Business at the University of California-Irvine. The goal of this five-year endeavor has been to answer this one very big question:

How can the modern executive team strategically and tactically manage through the various recessionary and expansionary phases of the business cycle to gain competitive advantage over rivals?

The quite literally hundreds of companies analyzed to answer this compelling question run the gamut from well-known behemoths, such as DuPont and Citigroup, that staff their own teams of economists and use their own sophisticated forecasting models to much smaller niche players, such as Isis and Xilinx, that few have heard of—but many executives can learn from. These companies also span the globe—from the Mexican cement giant CEMEX and high-flying Singapore Airlines to the boutique Chinese real estate entrepreneur SOHO China.

Chapter 1 provides a brief overview of the concept of Master Cyclist management and the high stakes involved in managing— or *mis*managing—the business cycle. Chapters 2 through 10 then use a host of highly entertaining real-world examples to illustrate each of the well-timed strategies and tactics of the Master Cyclist executive.

Having established the overriding importance of managing the business cycle, I illustrate in Chapter 11 how any business executive can learn to be his or her own economic forecaster using a relatively simple set of "off-the-shelf" forecasting tools and "leading economic indicators."

I hope, then, that you will enjoy this book as much as I have enjoyed researching and writing it. It truly offers a treasure trove of managerial insights. These are not mine but rather those of the finest strategic minds running some of the best companies in the world.

On behalf of the hundreds of members of the research team who contributed to the Master Cyclist Project (described in Appendix A), I can therefore confidently echo these words of the author of *Good to Great*, Jim Collins, who, in similar circumstances, had this to say:

Our five-year quest yielded many insights, a number of them surprising and quite contrary to conventional wisdom, but one giant conclusion stands above the others: We believe that almost any organization can substantially improve its stature and performance, perhaps even become great, if it conscientiously applies the framework of ideas we've uncovered.

CHAPTER

Strategies and Tactics of the Master Cyclist Executive

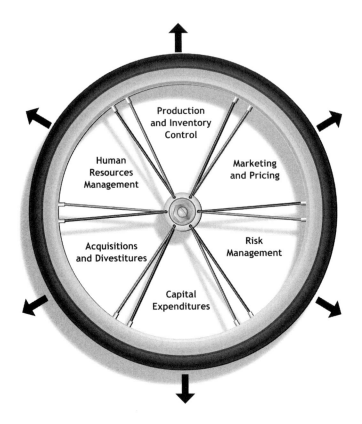

"The brightest people in the world didn't see [the recession] coming."

—John Chambers, CEO, Cisco Systems

"We saw this recession coming three years ago. It was obvious the booming economic cycle couldn't continue. We tightened our belts. We focused on cash flow."

—Ralph Larsen, CEO, Johnson & Johnson

Timing is everything. In love and war, most certainly. But certainly also in managing the business cycle.

Consider, for example, a "Master Cyclist" CEO such as Johnson & Johnson's Ralph Larsen, who studiously follows key leading economic indicators, who accurately anticipates an approaching recession, and then implements an appropriately "well-timed strategy." His executive team begins to cut production and trim inventories—even as his rivals are upping theirs. His team might also better be able to "right size" the company through more timely layoffs—even as rivals continue to add workers at premium wages. Nor, as Larsen's quotation suggests, will such an executive team embark on an overly aggressive capital expansion program at a time when cash flow is likely soon to begin falling and borrowing costs are at their highest.

In anticipation of the 2001 recession, Larsen's J&J did indeed boldly cut its capital expenditures by more than $100 million at the height of the economic boom in 2000—the first decrease in seven years. As J&J significantly built up its cash reserves, the company saw double-digit growth in both revenues and earnings. These positive indicators coupled with a "sector rotation" by investors into defensive sectors such as health and medical care stocks as the bear market took hold helped give J&J's stock a double-digit boost in both 2000 and 2001—and allowed Larsen to turn over the CEO reins in 2002 with his head held high.

In contrast, consider a brilliant but nonetheless "Reactive Cyclist" CEO such as John Chambers of Cisco. Lacking the appropriate "business cycle literacy," Chambers failed to read numerous signs that the March 2001 recession was on its way—from a doubling of oil prices and a flattening yield curve in 1999 to a collapsing stock market and dramatically rising interest rates in 2000. Chambers also presided over a company that, by its very organizational design, lacked many macroeconomic variables in its business cycle forecasting models. As one Cisco top executive put it, "The economy is too complex to get anything meaningful out of such broad numbers as GDP or interest rates."[1]

Is it any wonder that Cisco got caught flat-footed in the 2001 recession and was eventually forced to write off more than $2 *billion* in excess inventory—even as the company had to lay off more than 8,000 people. While J&J's stock price was soaring, Cisco's came crashing back to earth.

Using a wealth of real-world examples involving some of the most successful—and hapless!—companies in the world, this book examines the startling contrast between the well-timed strategies and tactics of business cycle-savvy executives like Larsen versus the ill-timed and ill-considered reactions of executives like Chambers.

You will see that while Master Cyclist companies like J&J routinely achieve superior performance using these well-timed strategies and tactics over the course of the business cycle, Reactive Cyclist companies like Cisco often both literally and routinely hemorrhage cash *and* people during recessions—and, in the worst case, go bankrupt.

■■ ■ The Master Cyclist Management Wheel

"The essence of strategy is to achieve a long-term advantage over the firm's competitors."

—Professor Arnoldo Hax, Sloan School of Management

The Master Cyclist management "wheel" illustrated in Figure 1-1 provides an overview of the well-timed strategies and tactics that have been shown to be the most effective by some of the very best strategists running some of the very best companies in the world. These strategies and tactics encompass not just the key functional areas of marketing and pricing, production and inventory control, and human resource management. They also target the all-important areas of risk management, the strategic implementation of capital expenditure programs, and the tactical timing of acquisitions and divestitures.

Accordingly, this management wheel spans virtually every major activity of the modern corporation, and a solid understanding and careful study of the well-timed strategies and tactics arrayed in this wheel will help any business executive team dramatically improve company performance.

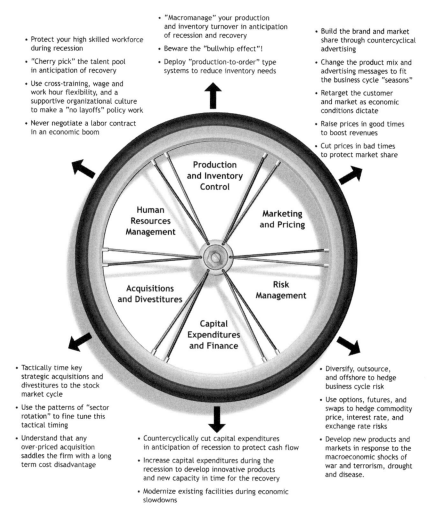

▲ **FIGURE 1-1** *Well-timed strategies and tactics of the Master Cyclist executive.*

Countercycling Your Capital Expenditures

The J&J example has already briefly highlighted the virtues of countercyclically *cutting* capital expenditures in anticipation of recession. This is a prudent *defensive* strategy that preserves cash flow at a most opportune time.

However, the most proactive of Master Cyclist executive teams also use the countercycling of capital expenditures as a potent *offensive* weapon. This is done by *increasing* capital expenditures during a recession in anticipation of a recovery and renewed and surging demand.

In this countercyclical way, Master Cyclists can position their companies to take the market high ground when the recovery begins. As examples from the likes of Loews, Intel, and a fascinating real estate company known as SOHO China will teach us, they do this with an abundance of new production capacity, an expanded retail outlet network, new and innovative products, and/or the latest and lowest-cost production and supply chain technologies.

Strategically Timing Your Acquisitions and Divestitures

From a strategic perspective, there are many compelling reasons why one company acquires another. The acquisition might open new markets, or the acquired company might own a complementary new technology. It might be a crucial link in the supply chain or possess a key patent. Most Machiavellian, the acquisition target might simply be a key rival that needs to be eliminated if competition is to be reduced and prices are to be raised.

Still, from a Master Cyclist perspective, it *never* makes any sense to impulsively make an acquisition if the stock price is too high—no matter how compelling the strategic reason. That is why, as you will see with stellar examples from companies such as chipmaker Micron, telecom calling card King IDT, and the credit-scoring maven Fair Isaac, the acquisitive Master Cyclist executive team always uses its highly sophisticated understanding of the business and stock market cycles to tactically time any key acquisition or divestiture to the business cycle.

The Art of Cherry Picking and Other HRM Tactics

In the deep dark depths of a recession, the last thing many companies want to do is to hire more people. *Not* so for the Master Cyclist.

The Master Cyclist knows that it is precisely at the trough of a recession that the labor pool is at its deepest and highest quality. Moreover, any wage pressures will have totally subsided. That is why to the Master Cyclist, a recession is a great time to "cherry pick" the labor market.

In this way, the Master Cyclist executive team gains a critical competitive advantage precisely because, when the new expansion begins, it is able to deploy a more highly skilled work force with lower labor costs than its rivals. That is a strategy that you will see played to absolute perfection by companies such as Avon, Isis, and Progressive in industry sectors as disparate as cosmetics, biotechnology, and insurance.

Production and Inventory

As you already have seen in the Cisco example, companies that continue to increase their production and build up inventories as a recession approaches inevitably suffer in myriad ways. Most obviously, bloated inventories increase holding costs, leave a company more vulnerable to breakage and pilferage, and, in the worst-case scenario, result in costly inventory write-downs—as Cisco painfully learned.

There is, however, a far more subtle cost to mismanaging one's inventories as a recession approaches. As the examples of Gateway and Hewlett-Packard will stunningly illustrate, a large inventory overhang can also leave a company with obsolete or out-of-fashion products that then must be dumped at fire-sale prices—even as more nimble competitors swoop in to seize market share.

Bloating the inventory as a recession approaches is not, however, the only—or perhaps even the worst—sin of the Reactive Cyclist. Indeed, companies that fail to increase production and build inventories in anticipation of an economic recovery are often left at the starting gate by far more aggressive rivals. The result, very often, is a sudden loss of market share to more business cycle-sensitive Master Cyclist competitors able to quickly stock shelves and showrooms with the latest products and styles as the economy kicks once again into high gear.

Indeed, this is a highly dynamic "macromanaging" process that you will see played out in a marathon boxing match between two heavyweight truck manufacturers. In one corner will be the consummate Master Cyclist Paccar, with its incredible accordion-like ability to ramp down or ramp up its production at the first sign of recession or recovery. In the other corner will be the historically pitiful and pathetic Navistar, which has always been caught a day late and a dollar short over the course of the business cycle—and frequently knocked down and out by Paccar in the battle for profitability and market share.

Marketing and Pricing Through the Business Cycle Seasons

The strategic and tactical implications of Master Cyclist marketing and pricing offer some of the richest insights into building competitive advantage in all of management strategy. For example, as a "time capsule" example of what was then a very young and upstart Dell will illustrate, increasing advertising during a recession can be a highly effective way of building the brand and increasing market share. This is because during recessions, ad rates are at their cheapest, and there is far less competition and "noise" in the marketplace.

Paradoxically, despite compelling evidence that countercyclical advertising is a highly effective strategy, you will nonetheless see that many companies do just the opposite in a recession and severely slash advertising. This happens because the Reactive

Cyclist leaders at these companies inevitably succumb to the pressures of the company "bean counters" who will always find advertising expenditures to be one of the easiest and most inviting cost-cutting targets in the company's beleaguered recessionary budget. However, as Kmart's myopic "Mac the Knife" CEO will grimly illustrate, such a misplaced strategy can be a shortcut straight into Chapter 11 bankruptcy.

It is not just in the realm of countercyclically advertising that the Master Cyclist shines. Far more subtly, the Master Cyclist marketer is also adept at tactically changing both the marketing messages and product mix to fit the customer's changing "moods" across the business cycle seasons.

The simple truth behind such tactical cycling of the product mix and messages is that many consumers respond much more to product value than style in recessionary times. This is a point that will be driven home in high culinary style by the likes of the "Crazy Chicken"—the fast-food, flame-grilled chicken chain El Pollo Loco. The company's highly creative and cost-saving "dark meat gambit" in the darkest days of recession turned out to be one of the most wildly successful marketing promotions in the company's history.

Tactically Hedging Business Cycle Risk

The business cycle can be very risky business indeed. Accordingly, many companies choose to strategically deploy a variety of hedging tools such as futures and options to completely neutralize both general business cycle risk as well as the more specific macroeconomic risks associated with movements in commodity prices, interest rates, and exchange rates.

For example, the Master Cyclists at Royal Caribbean Cruise love to hedge the company's substantial exchange rate risk with currency futures when they buy billion-dollar ships in euros from Europe. So, too, will you see how a company such as Good Humor-Breyers always hedges the costs of its most important ingredients—from premium vanilla cultivated in Madagascar to premium-quality New Zealand butterfat for its heart-stopping ice cream brands. In this way, both Royal Caribbean and Good Humor-Breyers are able to focus on their "core competencies"— whether it be providing high-quality cruise experiences or the most tasty pint of Ben & Jerry's Cherry Garcia.

Still, you will see that the true mark of the Master Cyclist involves not just static strategic hedges to neutralize risk but also more proactive "tactical hedging" to opportunistically leverage such risk. This is a lesson to be learned from the likes of the utterly masterful Master Cyclists at Southwest Airlines who, unlike virtually all other airlines, have brilliantly and opportunistically adjusted their oil price hedges in response to forecasts from their own internal and highly sophisticated models.

Strategically Diversifying Business Cycle Risk

Beyond simple hedging instruments such as futures and options, the Master Cyclist deploys two other important risk management tools: *business unit diversification* and *geographical diversification*. Of course, just as with acquisition and divestiture strategies, there are many good strategic and synergistic reasons why a company might want to engage in business unit or geographical diversification that have *nothing* to do with managing business cycle risk and broader macroeconomic risk.

Consider that with *business unit diversification*, an automaker that diversifies into producing SUVs may be able to build larger manufacturing facilities and thereby realize "economies of scale" and lower unit costs. More subtly, if some parts and assemblies can be used in *both* cars and SUVs—shocks, brake drums, or engines— the vehicle maker can also realize "economies of scope" by jointly producing the two kinds of vehicles, each with lower costs.

That said, there are equally obvious benefits to various forms of business unit diversification that effectively do hedge business cycle risk. You will see, for example, how a highly astute Countrywide Financial executive team has created a "natural business model hedge" by having one business unit that focuses on mortgage loan originations and another that focuses on mortgage loan servicing. Because the revenues from these two businesses move in *opposite* directions with movements in interest rates, Countrywide is able to achieve more stable revenues over the course of the business cycle and related interest rate cycle.

As for *geographical diversification*, there are likewise many excellent reasons to engage in such a strategy that have nothing to do with hedging business cycle risk. For example, by diversifying into new foreign markets, companies can achieve greater economies of scale. They can also deploy their core managerial and production skills across a broader range of opportunities.

Still, these strategic benefits notwithstanding, it is equally true that one of the primary benefits of geographical diversification is to significantly reduce business cycle vulnerability. Such geographical diversification works because, as a matter of statistical truth, the business cycles and political conditions of various countries are not, as they say in academia, "perfectly correlated" statistically. In lay terms, this means that while Europe or Japan might be experiencing a recession, China or the United States might be in the midst of a robust expansion.

This is a point driven home in one of the most sophisticated and entertaining examples in the entire book. This example involves the giant Mexican cement manufacturer CEMEX and its bold, bargain-hunting foray into Indonesia and the Philippines during the chaos and confusion of the 1997 through 1998 Asian currency crisis meltdown.

From Random Shocks Come Profitable Opportunities

A new kind of dangerous urban combat in Iraq creates a lucrative opportunity for companies such as Ceradyne and Kyocera to hawk their ceramic body armor. Terrorism spawns huge new markets for products as diverse as bomb-detection equipment and biometric identification. Companies such as InVision and Viisage swoop in with new products to grab a lion's share. Bird flu sweeps across Asia and sets off a vaccine-development sweepstakes to the benefit of large companies such as MedImmune and smaller speculative ventures such as China's Sinovac. Is it any wonder that economics has been dubbed the "dismal science"?

Dismal and grim though these thoughts may be, the random shocks that can arise both from the madness of mankind and from the Mad Cow rampages of Mother Nature present both dangers and opportunities. Unfortunately, in the chaos that often ensues after a random shock, many executives are caught flat-footed.

Master Cyclists are, however, immediately able to parse both the tactical implications of such random shocks as well as their longer-term strategic opportunities. You will see these themes played out by a diverse cast of companies that deftly illustrate how to develop new products or retarget old markets in response to the ravages of randomness.

▰▰ An Old Classic Sets the Stage for Our Master Cyclist Beginning

"Knowing when to act is as important as knowing what to do."

—Lakshman Achuthan, Managing Director, Economic Cycle Research Institute

To end this chapter, I want to leave you with a highly compelling example from the slim but nonetheless important work of Professor John McCallum—one of the earliest advocates of managing the business cycle for competitive advantage. This story aptly sets the stage for the numerous examples to follow, even as it illustrates why, as Lakshman Achuthan of the Economic Cycle Research Institute asserts in the preceding excerpt, "knowing when to act" is strategically just as important as "knowing what to do":

> Retailer Montgomery Ward is the classic example of what can happen when an enterprise miscalculates the direction of the macroeconomy for too long and by too much. Believing that depression always followed a major war, chairman Sewell Avery did not open a new store between World War II and the mid-1950s. Sears took the opposite tack, opening new stores relentlessly, particularly in the fast-growing suburbs.
>
> Sears was betting on strong, post-war growth driven by pent-up demand. Sears took off; Montgomery Ward never really recovered and eventually filed for bankruptcy. Many factors were involved in the dramatically different post-war paths of these legendary Chicago retailing rivals. The crucial fact remains that one was right about the macroeconomic direction. The other was wrong.

In the chapters that follow, you will see this same kind of battle played out in myriad intricate ways as we use a treasure trove of real-world examples to systematically work our way through the Master Cyclist management wheel. In the course of what should be for you both a very interesting and highly entertaining journey, one abiding fact will stand out.

In an increasingly global and fiercely competitive economy, the line between corporate success and failure is now being drawn by the ability—or lack thereof—of the modern executive team to first understand the business cycle in all of its strategic and tactical richness and then proactively manage that cycle for competitive advantage.

Countercycling Your Capital Expenditures

"... though a countercyclical investment strategy was observed to enhance profitability, few firms practiced this strategy."

—Professors David Aaker and Briance Mascarenhas[1]

Rather than profitably build up companies through the kind of "countercyclical investment strategy" described by Professors Mascarenhas and Aaker, many executive teams pursue just the opposite course. However, *nothing* can get a company into more trouble than ramping up an overleveraged capital-expansion program into the teeth of a recession. Such an overaggressive capital expansion creates large cash flow needs to service an ever-larger debt at a perilous time when revenues can fall dramatically.

This is exactly the kind of Reactive Cyclist cash flow squeeze that you will see companies such as Labor Ready, Gateway, and Calpine encounter—in large part because of the hubris of their own executive teams. In stark strategic contrast, you will also see why a "defensive specialist" such as DuPont provides a stellar Master Cyclist example of preemptively and countercyclically reducing capital expenditures in anticipation of a recession.

Still, the most important well-timed capital-expenditure strategy in the Master Cyclist repertoire may well be the one that you will see practiced so well in the examples of Intel, Lowe's, and, most exotically, the Chinese real estate developer SOHO China. This strategy is to countercyclically invest heavily in the middle of a recession when interest rates are low and credit is plentiful. The goal: strongly position one's company for the next recovery with an abundance of new and innovative products.

The Credit-Crunch Dangers of Overexpanding into a Recession

- Labor Ready's CEO "confuses brains with a bull market," overexpands into a recession, and brings down himself and (almost) his company.
- A morally challenged "whiz kid" MBA leads the once lean and mean Gateway to commit business model hari-kari by opting for an ill-advised, and exceedingly ill-timed, retail outlet strategy.
- Calpine's Pinocchio CEO succumbs to a classic "build the empire" syndrome by choosing the worst possible time to try to "repower North America"—and learns how to spell "junk bond."

"A recession attacks the life blood of a company—its cash flow..."

—Professor Richard Nolan, Harvard Business School

"Don't confuse brains with a bull market" is a wise old Wall Street proverb that has an important corollary in strategic management. During prolonged economic booms, far too many top executives come to think of themselves as brilliant captains of industry rather than simply well-talented individuals who also happen to find themselves very much in the right industry with the right product at the right economic time. But here's the very big problem.

When top executives confuse their own management skills with the conditions of a "do no wrong" boom, they can easily fall prey to a classic "build the empire syndrome." They continue to forge ahead with ever-larger expansion plans—oblivious to the possibility that, just as when the stock market suddenly goes bearish for a heavily margined investor, it can all come crashing down in a credit crunch.

Labor Ready Misses Its Own Recessionary Signals

> *"Labor Ready has been a victim of its own success. Exploding from 200 branch offices in 1996 to more than 800 in 2001, the company overreached. As chief executive, Mr. Welstad 'became intoxicated with the echo from Wall Street of his rhetoric'..."*
>
> **—The Economist**

This excerpt aptly captures how the wildly overaggressive capital expansion of a CEO "intoxicated" by his company's past success drove Labor Ready into deep trouble.

Labor Ready is the "McDonald's" of the day-labor world. Its army of roughly 600,000 manual laborers is dispatched every day from offices both in the United States and Puerto Rico as well as Canada and Great Britain to perform some of the most backbreaking and dangerous jobs on the planet.

There is a supreme irony to a company such as Labor Ready falling on its own capital-expansion sword. That's because Labor Ready should have been one of the first to anticipate the recession and *never* should have fallen into the classical overexpansion trap. Why is this so?

The demand for temporary labor is, in and of itself, a very good "coincident indicator" of economic activity. That is, as an economy softens, corporations will need fewer temporary workers, and as an economy expands, the demand for temps will increase. In light of the real-time labor-demand data quite literally at their fingertips, it is nothing short of incredible to see how badly CEO Welstad and his executive team—with their thumbs so close to the pulse of the economy—botched the company's aggressive capital-expansion strategy.

This unforgivable stumble would leave Labor Ready operating right in the middle of the 2001 recession with a record number of branches and soaring operating costs—just as the bottom was falling out of its business. Predictably, as year-over-year sales declined sharply in both 2001 and 2002 amid these rising costs, the company was forced to close about 150 of its offices—many of which, I hasten to add here, should never have been opened.

In a bit of poetic justice, not just Labor Ready's shareholders suffered mightily as Labor Ready's stock fell from around $15 per share at the beginning of 2000 to a little more than $3 per share as the March 2001 recession began. Welstad, himself, wound up losing his job in the most ironic of ways: He took an unauthorized loan from the company to meet a margin call on the crumbling Labor Ready stock he had bought on the big—but exceedingly bad—bet it would keep going up.

When the stock plummeted, Welstad found himself with a massive loss he could not cover. This is stark testimony to the fact that Welstad managed to "confuse brains with a bull market" not once but twice—once with his company and again with his own investment portfolio.

Gateway Commits Cap-Ex Hari-Kari

> *"Sure, we might have started out as a direct, built-to-order PC maker [like Dell], but Ted's vision was always bigger than that."*

—Jeff Weitzen, CEO, Gateway, 1999 Annual Report

> *"Let's face it. 2002 wasn't a very good year."*

—Ted Waitt, CEO, Gateway, 2002 Annual Report

This juxtaposition of quotations tells a sad and sordid tale of a company that frittered away literally billions of dollars of shareholder wealth by rolling the dice on a costly, ill-conceived, and ultimately arrogant retail outlet expansion strategy under the assumption that the "good economic times" would never end.

The Gateway example is, however, more than just a cautionary tale of an overaggressive capital-expenditure program into the teeth of an expansionary bubble. It is an equally compelling story about why it can be very dangerous to surrender your company to the leadership of a young, ethically challenged, hotshot MBA grad who has little or no concept of how to deftly manage a company through the business cycle.

This Gateway story begins in classic humble-beginnings style in 1985. In a small farmhouse, college dropout Ted Waitt started a solely build-to-order personal computer business that relied upon Dell's *direct distribution* model of business—long before Dell made it so famous! With this lean and efficient business model, the dropout Waitt fortuitously hit the exact sweet spot of what was then the unfolding computer boom. And Gateway did indeed boom—hitting the $1 billion in revenues mark by 1992 and the $5 billion mark by 1996.

Note, however, that by 1999, Waitt had become a more philanthropically oriented billionaire tired of running in the PC rat race. At this critical point in the computer industry cycle, he turned the CEO responsibilities over to Jeffrey Weitzen. Weitzen was a young, aggressive entrepreneur who proudly touted his University of Chicago MBA pedigree and who, much more important, wanted to put his own visionary stamp on Gateway.

You can see Weitzen's hubristic vision clearly in Gateway's 1999 Annual Report. In his chairman's statement, Weitzen delights in first tweaking the nose of Gateway competitor Dell as he implicitly mocks the Dell direct distribution model that Gateway had, in fact, originally been built on. Instead, Weitzen favored a much bigger vision of an international *retail outlet* empire. And make no mistake about it, much like the *Titanic* in its time, Weitzen's vision was big.

From a base of 280 retail stores in 1999, Weitzen would grow Gateway to a peak of almost 400 of its "Countrywide" retail stores in little more than a year. At the same time, Weitzen would add almost 700 new "stores within stores" as part of a $50 million investment in the office supply company OfficeMax.

A press account in *Business Week* of exactly how that OfficeMax deal came to be signed reveals the highly secretive nature of Weitzen's "one-man" executive band:

> *"Tanned, trim, and soft-spoken, Weitzen seems like a laid-back, southern-California sort of guy. Don't believe it. He's so obsessed with his job that he closed a huge deal to locate Gateway outlets within OfficeMax Inc. stores during a family vacation—sitting poolside at The Phoenician in Scottsdale, Ariz. 'Thanks to my cell phone and laptop, I don't think anybody knew,' he says."*

Not content to stop with his massive retail outlet expansion in the United States, Weitzen's Gateway also continued to aggressively expand into both Europe and Asia. Unfortunately, all these expansionary moves added significant overhead costs to a Gateway balance sheet at precisely the time when the computer industry "good times" were about to be very over.

Gateway's fall from direct distribution grace can be best measured by a performance yardstick called the SG&A ratio. It compares "selling, general, and administrative" expenses compared to total revenues.

In 1994, Gateway, with its direct distribution model, had one of the lowest SG&A ratios in the industry—a mere 7 percent. By the end of Weitzen's ill-timed expansion, that ratio had ballooned to more than twice that amount—comparable to the likes of Apple and Compaq but soaring high above the 9 percent of Dell—the company that Weitzen's had so arrogantly needled in his 1999 expansionary blueprint.

Predictably, as the 2001 recession took hold, Gateway was left high and dry with high inventory levels clogging its retail channels and falling gross margins unable to support its higher overhead model. As even Weitzen himself was forced to admit as Gateway began to badly miss its earnings estimates, there is "a lot of inventory rotting on the shelves."

There is an interesting "just desserts" *coup de grâce* to this retail outlet meltdown. With its own distribution channels as unclogged as a teenage heart, Dell smelled Gateway's blood in the water. In true Master Cyclist fashion, Dell began lowering its prices to spur demand and to tear off large chunks of Gateway's now falling market share.

At this point, Weitzen summarily got the ax when Gateway's founder Ted Waitt came back to try to rescue the company. Unfortunately, the college dropout did not do much better than the MBA—at least in the near term.

By the end of 2001, Gateway had just 7 percent of the computer market—a 60 percent drop in market share. But that was not the worst news. By December 2001, Gateway stock had lost 80 percent of its value, while almost half of Gateway employees were forced to hit the unemployment line.

Perhaps the final lesson to be learned from Gateway's roll of the capital-expansion dice is that mismanaging the business cycle in an ethical vacuum can not only severely damage a company. It can also get you into big trouble with the law.

In November 2003, the whiz kid Weitzen, along with Gateway's former CFO and controller, were charged by the Securities and Exchange Commission for "engaging in a fraudulent earnings-manipulation scheme to meet Wall Street analysts' expectations" as Gateway's fortunes fell dramatically in 2000. Fortunately for Weitzen and his cronies, Waitt stepped in quickly to settle the case with the starkly amusing promise that Gateway would never cook its books again. As for Weitzen—and the perversity of justice in the corporate world—he was rewarded for his incompetence with a $5.6 million severance payment.

Calpine Bets the Farm

> *"2001 was the most tumultuous year the power industry has ever faced. In spite of this, it was a great year for Calpine ... Most important, Calpine's business model has been validated..."*

> **—Peter Cartwright, CEO, 2001 Annual Report**

In this allegedly "great year," Calpine's stock mimicked a meteor disintegrating toward Earth as it fell from more than $50 a share to less than $10. Meanwhile, Calpine's bond rating went from near-blue-chip status to outright junk. It is difficult to understand how such an abominable performance could lead any rational CEO to assert that the "business model has been validated."

In fact, the story of the San Jose, California-based Calpine is interesting not just because it illustrates the liquidity dangers of an overaggressive capital-expansion strategy. It also helps to emphasize how individual patterns of so-called *sector rotation* (explained more fully in Chapter 11, "The Master Cyclist's Favorite Forecasting Tools") in the stock market can prove useful in forecasting movements in the business cycle—even as this sordid little Reactive Cyclist tale reveals how CEOs often try to lie to their shareholders to cover their own mistakes.

To understand more clearly the predictive power of sector rotation, let's look more closely at what Calpine does. This is a company that builds large, natural-gas-fired electricity generators and then sells that electricity in the wholesale market to electric utilities for distribution to their retail customers.

From a sector-rotation point of view, the electricity-generation sector sits in the broader energy category, and energy prices tend to peak in the Late Bull phase of the stock market cycle. In this phase, the business cycle is typically in its late and often red-hot expansionary stage when energy supplies are tight and energy demand is high. However, higher energy prices coupled with rapidly growing inflationary pressures and rising interest rates are destined to soon bring the economy crashing back down to Earth.

This late expansionary stage is, of course, absolutely the worst possible time for an energy or electricity company to undertake an aggressive capital-expansion program. When the business cycle turns down, energy prices will typically soften very swiftly and depress both cash flow and profits in the face of overcapacity and cutthroat competition, which can leave an aggressively expanding company extremely vulnerable to serious liquidity concerns.

This is precisely how Calpine and its Pinocchio CEO got into so much trouble. In February 2001, a full 11 months after the yield curve had inverted to signal recession (as explained more fully in Chapter 11) and just 1 month before the recession would begin, CEO Cartwright announced that he was upping Calpine's capital-expansion target to an astonishing 70,000 megawatts of electricity-generating capacity by 2005. This was from a base of less than 10,000 megawatts. It was an expansion that would be the equivalent of building more than *fifty* new nuclear power plants and would make Calpine the largest power producer in the country.

Unfortunately, as the recession took hold, Calpine predictably began to suffer what would become a severe reduction in cash flow to service its now roughly $14 billion of debt. Here is how this cash flow squeeze was described in *Business Week* on the one-year anniversary of Cartwright's bold promise to "repower" North America:

"Today, Calpine is powering down fast. ... It's reeling from falling electricity demand caused by the recession and from the debts it racked up to fund new plants. Calpine faces uncertainty about its liquidity and expansion strategy. We're questioning its ability to stay financially viable until an economic recovery comes..."

It is well worth commenting here on one of the many attempts by Cartwright at misdirection in the company's annual reports. In this particular instance, Cartwright tried to blame the Enron scandal and the use of "more conservative standards across the power industry" for the company's junk bond status rather than accept responsibility for succumbing to the classic "build the empire" syndrome.

Perhaps the most amazing thing is that after this bonehead Reactive Cyclist move, Cartwright kept his job. This was even as Calpine stock fell deep into penny-stock territory.

■■■ Protecting Cash Flow Through Countercyclical Retrenchment

■ Taking a page right out of J&J's playbook, DuPont's highly sophisticated forecasting team pays shareholders big dividends as the company prospers by cutting back on capital expenditures in anticipation of the recession.

"We saw this recession coming three years ago. It was obvious the booming economic cycle couldn't continue. We tightened our belts. We focused on cash flow."

—Ralph Larsen, CEO, Johnson & Johnson

You might recall Larsen's quotation from the first chapter in this book. It succinctly describes J&J's prescient capital-expenditure retrenchment in the face of a looming recession. This turned out to be an astute countercyclical defensive measure that helped lead J&J to superior performance over the course of the recession. Next, you will see how the chemical giant DuPont managed to pull off a similar feat.

DuPont's Sophisticated Forecasting Team Provides the Cash Flow Edge

"Because of the nature of our business, DuPont was one of the first to see the economic troubles on the horizon. We made immediate adjustments to deal with recession even as debate continued about whether the United States was headed for one."

—Chad Holliday, CEO, 2001

The Master Cyclist DuPont is one of the few major corporations in America to still have a staff of its own economists. It also has a very sophisticated macroeconomic forecasting model that has proved to be of great value in strategic decision making, and the company also subscribes to a number of forecasting services such as those of the Economic Cycle Research Institute.

Perhaps not surprisingly given these resources, DuPont's economists were projecting as early as 1999 that GDP growth would soon be slowing down from its very strong rates. By 2000, this team sensed trouble as they forecasted "weakness in the apparel and motor vehicle markets and slower growth in the construction industry—which are end-use markets for over 40 percent of the company's sales."

With a possible recession looming, DuPont's executive team swiftly moved into action. A major strategic thrust was to countercyclically ratchet down the company's capital expenditures—taking these expenditures from almost $7 billion in 2000, to just more than $2 billion in 2001, as the recession was taking hold.

Because it acted so quickly and defensively on this and several other fronts, DuPont was able to build a large cash reserve. As

Business Week described the company's enviable deep-pocket status, DuPont was thus able to position itself as "among 20 companies with the financial strength and flexibility to take advantage of bear market acquisition opportunities."

In fact, throughout 2001, and in a Master Cyclist theme we explore much more fully in the next chapter, DuPont used its cash hoard to make fully *seven* highly strategic acquisitions. These acquisitions—mostly at bargain prices in the midst of the recession—would give DuPont a set of valuable new technologies to drive deeply into important future growth markets as the recovery took hold.

As a result of its aggressive and well-timed strategies, DuPont maintained profitability during the 2001 recession for all quarters except the second—no small feat for a highly cyclical chemical company.

▓▓■ The All-Important Well-Timed Countercyclical Expansion

- Intel's counter(cyclical) culture leads it to dramatically increase its capital expenditures during the recession while rivals are cutting back, and the company rides prosperously into the new economic recovery with new products blazing.
- Lowe's CEO obeys one of the most important Master Cyclist commandments—Know Thy Sector—and leaves the Reactive Cyclist Home Depot in the home-improvement dust.
- Real estate market wizard SOHO China shows us exactly why Master Cycling is as much a universal global phenomenon as it is a tool for both large and small businesses.

"I see an unparalleled opportunity to gain market share and expand business. The downturn has left some of our very heavily leveraged competitors weak and unable to invest in their businesses. By investing, we're a leg up and in better position to get new business or take away existing business from somebody else."

—King Harris, president and CEO, Pittway Corporation

We have seen that countercyclically cutting capital expenditures into the teeth of a recession to preserve cash flow is a very important defensive measure of the Master Cyclist. Where the true Master Cyclist goes on the offensive is through the implementation of a well-timed countercyclical expansion to prepare for the next recovery.

The Intel story illustrates how such proactive thinking is part of the very fabric and culture of the company, whereas the Lowe's example showcases how knowing one's own "industry cycle" is just as important as cultivating an awareness of the broader business cycle. To finish this chapter with a bit of international flair, the real estate developer SOHO China illustrates how strategic Master Cycling is as much a universal global phenomenon as it is a tool for both large and small businesses.

Intel's Counter(cyclical) Culture

"Recessions always end and innovation allows some companies to emerge from them stronger than before."

—Gordon Moore, co-founder, Intel

"The industry has shrunk more in the last two years than in any other down cycle ... But Intel plans to keep investing. That way we have huge strategic advantage when the markets inevitably recover."

—Paul Otellini, COO, Intel

An aggressive countercyclical capital-expenditure strategy to fuel product innovation has been the absolute bedrock of chipmaker Intel's corporate philosophy and culture. This is a company that over the course of its very profitable history has used the occasions of recessions and downturns in the semiconductor cycle to continually develop new products and better position itself for the next expansion. The opportunities provided by the 2001 recession proved to be no exception to Intel's countercyclical rule.

As many of its competitors were retrenching during the downturn, Intel continued to expand both its product line and its production facilities on several fronts. It not only opened up new plants and increased its production capabilities in many of its existing plants. Intel also invested heavily in two new technologies that would pay off handsomely when the recovery began.

In this innovative vein, Intel went both "jumbo" and "microscopic." On the jumbo front, it began using a manufacturing process that makes semiconductors on "jumbo" 300-millimeter (or 12-inch) wafers rather than the industry standard of 200-millimeter (8-inch) wafers. This new jumbo wafer makes twice as many chips and, in doing so, shaves 30 percent off the costs of cut-die manufacturing.

On the "microscopic" front, Intel embraced a 0.13-micron technology that shrinks transistor feature sizes. This new technology allows Intel to make high-performance chips that are smaller and faster. These chips also cost less to manufacture and even less to operate because they use less power. CEO Craig Barrett and Chairman Andy Grove described Intel's countercyclical strategy and culture in the 2001 Annual Report:

> [W]e know that a downturn is no time to shy away from strategic spending. Though the high-tech industry was mired in overcapacity in 2001, we know from experience that capacity wilts like lettuce. There's always too much of yesterday's technology and never enough of tomorrow's. … Consequently, during this downturn, we did what may seem counterintuitive: We accelerated our capital investments, spending $7.3 billion in 2001, compared with approximately $10 billion in capital spending over the previous two years combined. We also invested $3.8 billion in research and development 2001.…

The payoff from Intel's "counterintuitive" strategy was a handsome one. When the 2002–2003 recovery rolled around, Intel was able to quickly and quite successfully launch new products such as its new Centrino mobile processor technology and its highly touted Mobile Pentium IV-M processor. As it did so, Intel trumpeted loudly the great gains in performance, great savings in power consumption, and greater longevity for laptop computer batteries.

The undeniable result: Intel had a banner year in 2003 as revenues increased by 13 percent over 2002 and net income rose by 81 percent. Moreover, in the third quarter of 2003, as its new products swarmed into the market, Intel reported its highest rate of growth since the boom year of 1996.

Lowe's Obeys the "Know Thy Sector" Commandment

"When the economic climate changes, the world's best retailers look for opportunity. The marked economic shift that occurred during the latter part of 2000 was one such time, and Lowe's took the opportunity to evaluate our business and sharpen our vision for the future. ... Looking to the future, we see a fast-growing and highly fragmented $400 billion home-improvement industry only getting better."

—Robert Tillman, CEO, Lowe's, 2000 Annual Report

It's not just in the high-tech stratosphere of leading-edge semiconductor design and manufacturing where a strategy of countercyclical expansion can bear fruit. It is also in the more-down-to-bricks-and-mortar world of the home-improvement retailing sector. Exhibit A: the strong challenge of the Lowe's Corporation to the preeminence of Home Depot as the 2001 recession took hold.

This example underscores the importance of an executive team not only understanding how the business cycle moves. It also highlights the importance of understanding how the cycle of one's own particular *industry* sector moves in and out of phase with that broader business cycle.

Lowe's rise to power rightly begins in the last-gasp heat of the economic expansion of 2000. This was a time when CEO Robert Tillman firmly believed that the time was ripe to make Lowe's a national player on the home-improvement scene. As Tillman put it in the preceding excerpt, "When the economic climate changes, the world's best retailers look for opportunity."

So what exactly did Tillman and his executive team see in what Tillman described as a "marked economic shift" that archrival Home Depot didn't? Well, Tillman clearly believed that the economy would peak in 2000—a correct but very contrarian view at the time. But Tillman also foresaw a multiple-stage industry-adjustment process that would greatly benefit his business when the recession hit.

This process would involve first a recession in which home remodeling and repairs would increase as new home sales sagged. Then, in the next stage, as the Federal Reserve lowered interest rates, this would further fuel home remodeling as consumers refinanced their homes and used the drawn-out equity funds for even more expensive remodeling. Finally, lower interest rates would then spur a new housing boom for the next growth leg up for Lowe's stores.

Tillman's highly sophisticated Master Cyclist analysis did not stop there, however. Lowe's also was counting on playing an important macroeconomic *demographic* card. As Tillman observed in that 2000 Annual Report blueprint for overtaking Home Depot:

> *The home-improvement market is expected to grow over 4 percent annually for the next four years, as Baby Boomers trade up, remodel, and generally improve their homes, and [Generation] X'ers buy and move into their first homes and prepare for the family to follow.*

On the basis of this Master Cyclist logic, Lowe's embarked in 1999 on a strategy to open almost 300 new stores by the end of 2001.

At this point, you might be thinking that this kind of capital expansion into the teeth of a recession looks a lot more like the profligate Reactive Cyclism of companies such as Gateway and Labor Ready than the kind of prudent "battening down the hatches" capital-expenditure cutbacks that we observed—and praised in this chapter—with companies such as DuPont and J&J. In fact, on the face of it, Tillman's aggressive plan does seem much more suited for a ride along the road to junk bond ruin taken by the likes of Calpine and Peter Cartwright. However, this is where it is very important to reiterate how important it is for business executives to understand clearly the particular sector they operate in and how that sector is affected not just by the business cycle but also by the highly related interest rate cycle and other factors such as the aforementioned changing demographics.

The really crucial point to make in this regard is that during recessionary times, as in 2001, demands for Labor Ready's workers, Gateway's computers, and Calpine's electricity will indeed all go into the toilet. However, in such times, as noted above, *the home-improvement market can actually grow and prosper.* That's why Know Thy Sector is one of the top 10 commandments of every Master Cyclist.

Here is how the adjustment process that Tillman envisioned actually unfolded: Interest rates did indeed continue to rise and housing starts dropped in 2000 just as one would expect leading into recession. Although this temporarily squeezed Lowe's, by the latter half of 2000, the Federal Reserve finally began lowering short-term interest rates, and the 30-year fixed mortgage rates followed—just as Tillman had anticipated.

At that point, Lowe's business began to boom. By the first quarter of 2001, profits were a very respectable $149 million. By the third quarter, 2002 net income increased to almost $500 million—even as Lowe's began to grab an ever-bigger slice of market from Home Depot. By 2003, the news was even better, as evidenced by this excerpt from CNNMoney.com:

> *Lowe's Cos. reported improved fiscal fourth-quarter results Monday that beat the most optimistic forecasts from Wall Street. Shares of Lowe's jumped more than 4 percent in early trading on the New York Stock Exchange. The company … has been picking up market share from Home Depot, and the fourth quarter marks the eighth straight quarter it has topped analysts' forecasts.*

Now, it might be useful to note here that during this time of Lowe's ascendancy, Home Depot had gone into a classic defensive Reactive Cyclist mode. Under the new stewardship of former General Electric top executive Robert Nardelli, Home Depot focused its efforts not on an aggressive capital expansion like Lowe's but rather on ruthless cost-cutting measures, boosting the company's inventory turnover rate, improving its broader supply chain management, and squeezing its suppliers for discounts during the soft economic times.

So here's the irony: It is only after Nardelli and his bean-counting crew come to understand in 2003 just how the Lowe's capital-expansion bus had just ran over them that they belatedly ramp their own cap ex back up. Here's how CNNMoney.com reported this irony on the exact same February day that the Lowe's good earnings news broke:

> *Home Depot, the No. 1 U.S. home improvement retailer, lowered its sales and earnings growth targets for the coming fiscal year Friday, citing a challenging economic environment. … Home Depot … also said it is increasing capital spending by 21 percent to $4 billion to enhance the customer shopping experience and boost its sagging sales. …*
>
> *"We have embarked on a transformation of The Home Depot from a young, decentralized business toward a more mature and balanced company with predictable and sustainable growth potential," said Bob Nardelli, chairman, president and CEO of The Home Depot.*

Forgive me, but what a Reactive Cyclist crock. Here we have an outfoxed, old-school CEO using a misleading description of his number one company in the home-improvement market as a "young, decentralized business" as a lame justification for launching a capital-expenditure strategy that would be two to three years too late to stay ahead of its closest competition.

That, however, is precisely the kind of calamity that can strike when a "stranger in a strange land" executive such as Nardelli is imported into an industry in which he has little experience and really doesn't understand. To put this problem another way, although Nardelli's methods during the recession might have been well suited to his old company, he was out of his depth as soon as he jumped over into the home retailing business. Boards of directors, please take note of this point the next time you seek to hire top talent from outside your sector.

SOHO China's Master Cyclist Entrepreneur

"As a developer, we need to be a smart thinker, analyze the market trend wisely."

—Pan Shiyi, CEO, SOHO China

This SOHO China example properly begins in 1990 in the Chinese province of Hainan. Hainan is often referred to as the Chinese Hawaii because of its picturesque location on the south coast of China. But laid back like Hawaii, Hainan distinctly is not.

In fact, Hainan is an economic juggernaut, in large part because in 1990, the Chinese government designated Hainan a "special economic zone." In such zones, foreign investment is heavily subsidized, primarily through preferential tax policies and custom duties as well as by the removal of restrictions on foreign ownership of financial institutions.

For Hainan, the result of this special designation was a huge economic boom—and a collateral boom in real estate. In 1990 alone, more than $50 billion flowed into the Hainan real estate market.

In 1991, as a young developer speculating in the Hainan real estate market, Pan Shiyi saw one particular ratio—the construction-to-sales spread—start to widen. To Pan, this strongly suggested that the real estate market was beginning to overheat—a concern soon confirmed by a rapid rise in the price index. When Pan's customized indicators began to flash these danger signs, he, unlike most other developers in Hainan, pulled out of the market. As Pan put it, "The hot economy and beneficial local policies in Hainan attracted me to enter the Hainan market. However, in 1992, I found the real estate market was out of the economic pattern…"

Pan's timely withdrawal saved him from what has come to be known as the Hainan real estate shock of 1993. This was an almost total collapse of real estate prices that left many developers bankrupt and many banks loaded down with bad debt. But this was not to be Pan's only—or best—well-timed Master Cyclist move.

In 1995, Pan founded SOHO China, a small development company with a futuristic concept for Beijing. SOHO stands for "small office, home office." In promoting this futuristic concept, Pan's goal was to create a housing culture where Chinese entrepreneurs could live and work at the same place and where their living and working areas would blend seamlessly.

In 1997, to fully implement his SOHO vision, Pan began to systematically take advantage of yet another collapse in Chinese real estate prices, this time in Beijing. At this time, the Beijing real estate market was suffering both from the beginning throes of the 1997-1998 "Asian financial crisis" as well as the contractionary monetary policies of the Chinese government. In this environment of fear and tight money, demand for real estate declined sharply, investment shrank precipitously, and, in a trend that caught Pan's eye, land-acquisition costs fell sharply.

Surveying this seemingly bleak landscape, the Master Cyclist Pan saw two important factors at work that would motivate him to dive headlong into this beleaguered market. One was the healthy movement of a customized indicator he liked to follow known as the "savings index." It was signaling that savings were quickly rising, and with the rise in savings, people were accumulating significant amounts of cash—and purchasing power!

Second, as a very positive "regulatory shock" to the system, in 1998, the central government required all state-owned enterprises to stop "self-building" houses for employees and instead establish a housing financing system to facilitate private purchasing.

In this environment, Pan's SOHO engaged in significant land acquisitions to countercyclically build up the company's inventory. A few years later, the company brought its SOHO Newton project to market, and by 2001, this was the most popular project in Beijing, with almost $500 million in sales.

The broader result: By carefully following the real estate market with the help of several customized indicators and by countercyclically withdrawing from one market and then engaging in an aggressive capital-expenditure program to enter another, Pan Shiyi became one of the top 10 real estate developers in China within just 10 years.

Key Points

- **The Credit-Crunch Dangers of Overexpanding into a Recession**
  - Top executives whose companies prosper during boom times can easily fall prey to a "build the empire syndrome." They continue to ramp up an overleveraged capital-expansion program as a recession approaches. This creates large cash flow needs at a perilous time when revenues can fall dramatically.
- **Protecting Cash Flow Through Counter-cyclical Retrenchment**
  - Countercyclically cutting capital expenditures in anticipation of a possible recession is a very important defensive strategy employed by the Master Cyclist. It preserves cash flow at a most opportune time.
- **The All-Important Well-Timed Counter-cyclical Expansion**
  - A true Master Cyclist also goes on the market-share attack by countercyclically increasing capital expenditures during a recession. In this way, the company is ready with new capacity and new and innovative products when the recovery takes hold.

CHAPTER

3

The Acquisitive Master Cyclist Buys Low and Sells High

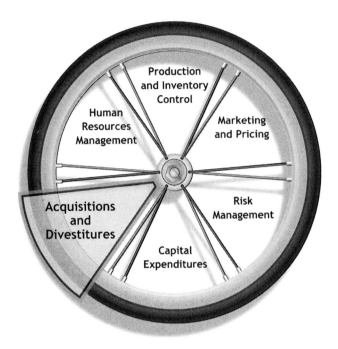

"What you try to do when you manage this type of company is broaden the franchise at the bottom of the (economic) cycle so that the snap out of the cycle can be positive. I think we really strengthened the company during this [recessionary] period."

—**Ronald DeFeo, CEO, Terex**

"We sold plants at the top when prices were at their peak. Now that everybody's selling, we're anxious to buy assets. It takes a hell of a lot of discipline, but sometimes you have to go against the market."

—**Richard Priory, CEO, Duke Power**

The age-old maxim "buy low, sell high!" is as true for a small investor laying down $500 for 100 shares of stock as it is for a large corporation shelling out $5 billion for a strategic acquisition.

From a strategic perspective, many compelling reasons induce one company to seek to acquire another. The acquisition target might open new markets or own a complementary new technology. The target might be a crucial link in the supply chain or possess a key patent. Most Machiavellian of all, the target might just be a key rival that needs to be eliminated if prices are to be raised.

Still, from a Master Cyclist perspective, it never makes any sense to impulsively make an acquisition if the stock price is too high—no matter how compelling the strategic reason. Nor does it make any sense to pay for any such acquisition by accumulating substantial debt at a time when interest rates are too high. That is why the acquisitive Master Cyclist always uses his highly sophisticated understanding of the business cycle—and the related stock market and interest rate cycles—to tactically time any key acquisition or divestiture.

▪▪▪ The "Buy High, Sell Low" Reactive Cyclist Blues

- ▪ Nortel Networks moves "at the speed of light" to consummate a series of extravagantly priced acquisitions—and vaporizes $75 billion in "market cap" for shareholders.
- ▪ Exodus Communications finances an acquisition spree with high-priced debt and winds up playing the cash-squeezed, bankrupt rabbit to the recessionary python.

In the euphoric white-hot heat of the late stages of an economic expansion, Reactive Cyclists turn the "buy low, sell high" rule completely on its head. Intoxicated by the bullish fumes—or perhaps spurred on by equally foolish rivals in a bidding war—they take the acquisition plunge at the worst possible time. This is a time when the irrationally exuberant bulls on Wall Street have driven stock prices up into "Dutch tulip craze" heights and, in response, a much more sober Federal Reserve has already begun to sharply drive up interest rates to curb incipient inflation.

In such heady times, your executive team must constantly remind itself that any overpriced acquisition will saddle your company with a long-term competitive cost disadvantage. Moreover, if your company takes on a heavy debt at high interest rates to finance a series of overpriced acquisitions—as you will now see both Nortel and Exodus did—it might face a major cash flow or bankruptcy problem as soon as a recession and new bear market hit.

Nortel Vaporizes $75 Billion in Market Cap

"We are moving at the speed of light to maintain our first mover advantage."

—John Roth, CEO, Nortel

The fiasco of telecom gear maker Nortel Networks puts an exclamation point on just how important it is to tactically time any set of strategic acquisitions to ensure that they are accretive—not destructive—to earnings.

In the late 1990s, Nortel faced a difficult strategic challenge. In the "old days" prior to the Internet revolution, all that Nortel's staid old phone company clients needed to build a telecom network was a bunch of wires and cable and some low-tech switches to route phone calls around.

The Internet revolution changed everything. As the number of Web users grew from a few million in 1995 to more than 200 million by 1999, both stodgy old phone companies such as AT&T and SBC along with a dizzying array of new companies such as Global Crossing and WorldCom all began demanding highly sophisticated gear. Such gear was needed to move not just voice over wire. It was also needed to move both voice *and* data over a flood of both wired *and* wireless "killer application" technologies.

With this astonishing technological revolution, a multi-*trillion*-dollar race for market share was on. This race would involve blending fiber optics, switchers, routers, Internet Protocol networking, wireless, and other rapidly emerging technologies into a system that would move "packets" of data and voice in the fastest and most cost-efficient manner possible.

In these frenetic times—often driven by the innovations of small start-up companies—Nortel embraced a strategy much like that of many other big gear makers, including Nortel's archrival Lucent. That is, Nortel rapidly sought to acquire strategic assets that would expand its product line and fill in all the technological blanks the company needed to fully service the Internet.

Nortel began to do this with what the company's lemming-like CEO described in the preceding excerpt as a dizzying "speed-of-light" pace. It executed no less than 12 major acquisitions in the 12 months leading up to the 2001 recession.

The problem with many of these acquisitions was not so much that they were not necessarily needed—although some of the more exotically named companies such as Alteon, Qtera, and Xros all turned out to be mostly busts that led to huge write-downs. Rather, in what had become the telecom industry's equivalent of an astonishingly expensive "arms race," the costs of acquiring these new companies had soared into the stratosphere; and, like a compulsive Las Vegas gambler, Nortel's executive team simply did not know when to quit.

Indeed, rather than looking forward like Master Cyclists at all the accumulating signals of the coming 2001 recession, the company's executive team kept looking over its shoulder at rivals such as Lucent and Cisco—worrying more about keeping pace with such rivals rather than providing real value to its shareholders.

Of course, the ultimate joke on shareholders was unusually cruel—the complete and utter vaporization of a staggering $75 *billion* in market capitalization. Nor were the more than 50,000-plus Nortel employees who lost their jobs wildly amused.

Still, anyone with any sense of humor at all has to see the statement of Nortel's CEO, John Roth, about *"moving at the speed of light to maintain our first mover advantage"* as darkly comic. For few companies have ever driven over such a big cliff at such a fast speed.

Predictably, in the 2001 Annual Report, Roth blamed the unforeseen recession for the company's collapse rather than the failure of the company's own leadership to anticipate the downturn. In classic Reactive Cyclist fashion, he referred to this rotten manna-from-hell event as a "sudden reversal of fortune that reverberated across the sector."

As the epilogue to this story, and in light of the pain he caused to employees and shareholders alike, it borders on the shameless that Roth was allowed to retire with more than a $100 million in cash—yet another clear sign of how the executive compensation and stock-option system rewards business cycle myopia.

Exodus Makes Its Exodus

"Exodus expanded rapidly by acquiring co-location and professional services firms American Information Systems and Cohesive Technology Solutions, as well as Service Metrics, a maker of Web site performance monitoring software, and 85% of Tokyo's Global Online Japan. The spending spree continued in 2000 with the purchase of e-business testing service provider KeyLabs and UK-based Grenville Consulting. The feather in the firm's cap was its acquisition of GlobalCenter, the Web-hosting unit of Global Crossing."

—Hoover's Online

At least Nortel survived its acquisition spree. Not so for another high-tech flyer: Exodus Communications. This is a company that began as a gleam in the eyes of several Indian entrepreneurs—K. B. Chandraskehar and B. V. Jagadeesh—and began to blossom on the shores of California in 1994.

The niche that Exodus sought to fill was "Web hosting." This service would allow Exodus clients to outsource their Internet operations to the company's so-called server farms. These high-capacity data centers would then be linked through a complex network involving both public and private channels of the Internet.

As Internet usage grew exponentially in the late 1990s, Exodus quickly became a *very* big business. It eventually grabbed a full quarter of the U.S. hosting market while running more than 40 data centers in eight countries on more than 2 million square feet of real estate.

This was a company, however, whose executive team had absolutely no Master Cyclist sense. How else can one explain the company's suicidal strategy of acquiring a bevy of companies with high-priced debt at the top of the interest rate cycle?

Of course, when the recession hit and the company's revenues declined dramatically, the interest payments on this huge debt squeezed Exodus's cash flow like a hungry python around a helpless rabbit. In the wake of an inevitable bankruptcy, the assets of this "rabbit" were soon swallowed up by two other companies: Cable & Wireless and Digital Island.

As with the Nortel example, this Exodus story also has a darkly amusing twist. For it was decidedly *not* the mistakes of the company's founders Chandraskehar and Jagadeesh that ultimately did the company in. Instead, in its exceedingly finite wisdom, the Exodus board of directors gave these entrepreneurs the boot and turned the reins of the company over to a more "experienced" CEO. She, like a college kid with her first credit card, promptly ran the company into the acquisitions ground. So much for "experience."

▦▪ Buying Low and Selling High—or Just Sitting It Out!

- A very cautious Integrated Device Technology refuses to chug the overpriced acquisitions Kool-Aid and winds up sitting the telecom meltdown out with a half billion dollars in cash. (IDT 1)

- IDT Corporation's iconoclastic CEO hits the "sell high" bull's eye by dumping Net2Phone shares to AT&T at the top of the market. Flush with cash, he then masterfully "buys low" to advance strategic objectives. (IDT 2)

- Micron's legendary CEO scoops up cheap semiconductor "fabs" at the bottom of the industry cycle to eliminate rivals and increase market share while cutting costs.

> *"... periods of economic decline can be occasions to buy rivals fairly quickly, consolidate market share, and get greater scale and competitive advantage."*
>
> **—Sol Berman, PwC Consulting**

From the lemming-like behavior of the Nortels and Exoduses of the telecom world, one might jump to the very wrong conclusion that *every* telecom executive was fooled by the recession. Yet clearly, for every naïve buyer of every wildly inflated company, there necessarily must also have been a savvy seller. That is why a central question we will keep asking is this: What distinguishes Master Cyclist leaders from the Reactive Cyclists? To gain further insight into this question, let's move on to a tale of "two telecom IDTs."

IDT #1 Selectively Sits It Out

> *"IDT was very cautious ... [R]ather than buying up a bunch of overpriced assets that didn't fit, we [were] very selective and ended up at the end of the downturn with a half-billion dollars net-of-debt in the bank."*
>
> **—Greg Lang, CEO, Integrated Device Technology**

The first IDT is more of a haiku than a full-fledged story. This IDT is "Integrated Device Technology." It's a Santa Clara, California-based company that fills a relatively small niche cranking out high-performance semiconductors and modules mostly for the telecom networking industry but also for the computer market.

With the brevity of a haiku, the preceding quotation from IDT's Greg Lang says it all. Rather than succumb to splurging on "overpriced assets that didn't fit," IDT sat on the sidelines, took far fewer lumps than its telecom brethren when the recession hit, and wound up counting its cash rather than chopping off executive heads.

IDT #2 Buys "Manhattan"

> *"IDT could stand for Invest in Distressed Telecom companies."*

> **—David Hamerly, Hoover's Online**

Our second IDT's situation is far more textured and nuanced. It illustrates an almost perfect mastery of both parts of the "buy low, sell high" approach to generate cash while advancing strategic objectives.

This second IDT is IDT Corporation. This is a company whose original claim to fame was to pioneer something known as "international callback technology." This "call re-origination" technology allowed IDT to reroute international calls through cheaper U.S. wires and thus avoid the high rates charged by overseas carriers. In this way, IDT could offer paid calling cards at bargain rates to connect its mostly lower-income and immigrant customer base to countries around the world.

Now here is what's interesting: Although IDT has made money through this call re-origination business, the really big bucks the company has generated have been the result of a series of brilliant "buy low, sell high" acquisition and divestiture deals engineered by IDT's founder and major shareholder—the often controversial and iconoclastic Howard Jonas.

Indeed, no executive has ever been able to hit the Master Cyclist bull's eye more squarely than Jonas did when he sold off a large stake in IDT's Internet telephony subsidiary Net2Phone. He unloaded almost 15 million shares of the company to the all-to-eager AT&T for a cool $1.4 billion in the very month the stock market hit its 2000 peak. This Master Cyclist *masterstroke* left IDT sitting in the middle of the recession at the very top of the telecom heap with no debt and no worries even as hundreds of other companies struggled to survive.

This is only part of the IDT story, however. Jonas did not just hoard his cash. Instead, during the trough of the 2001 recession, he went on his own acquisition spree, scooping up bargain assets with high strategic value at obscenely low prices.

For example, in February 2001, IDT swooped in to snatch his top phone card competitor PT-1 for just $26.1 million in cash—a tiny fraction of what PT-1 had been demanding just three months earlier. This elimination of a key rival allowed IDT to gain control of roughly a third of the prepaid calling card market, raise prices, boost revenues to the $1 billion mark, and achieve gross margins of more than 20 percent.

Still, the PT-1 acquisition was small change compared to IDT's acquisition of Winstar Government Solutions. This was a company with almost 60,000 federal customers and $200 million in annual revenues. It was also a company with a highly reliable "fixed wireless network" capable of delivering voice, video, data, and the Internet over the critical "last mile" to its customers. By providing last-mile capability, Winstar thus was an excellent fit with IDT's long-distance services.

Incredibly, the purchase price for Winstar was a mere $42.5 million—a company with almost $5 *billion* in assets. As if this bargain basement price weren't low enough, IDT paid for roughly a fourth of that price not with cash but with shares of its own stock. Crowed Jonas about this particular deal: "It might not top the Dutch settlers buying the island of Manhattan for $24, but it comes pretty close."

The Legendary Mr. Appleton Picks Some Low-Hanging Chips

"Micron has a record of making the most of adverse conditions. Thus, we have come through each market cycle stronger and more energized. We will pursue opportunities that arise from the current volatility and use them to advance our position."

—Steve Appleton, CEO, Micron

"Micron got a good deal there, 25 cents on the buck."

—Andrew Norwood, Gartner Research

The Micron story illustrates an almost perfect marriage between the dictates of sound corporate strategy telling us the "why" of an acquisition and the well-timed tactical implementation of that strategy telling us about the "when." The Micron story is also about a highly astute Master Cyclist executive who has perfected one simple strategy: *Purchasing chip fabrication facilities from competitors at the bottom of the semiconductor market cycle to eliminate rivals and increase market share while cutting costs and expanding production capabilities in anticipation of the next cyclical upturn.*

Micron is one of the world's leading semiconductor manufacturers of dynamic random access memory semiconductors—so-called DRAM chips. Micron's DRAM chips, together with its "Flash memory" chips, are used in everything from computers, workstations, and servers to cell phones, digital cameras, and even gaming systems.[1]

Micron's "living legend" CEO comes straight out of the pages of a Horatio Alger novel. Steve Appleton started out at Micron as a lowly nightshift line operator while still in college and worked his way up the entire chain of command.

By 1998, during a deteriorating DRAM market, Appleton's Micron scooped up four internationally dispersed semiconductor fabrications plants from Texas Instruments. These acquisitions geographically diversified Micron's chip production while at the same time eliminated significant capacity of a key rival.

In addition, in a provision whose importance was overlooked at the time by many analysts, Texas Instruments also agreed to allow Micron royalty-free use of its patents for a full 10 years. This gave Micron a very nice cost advantage over two of Micron's major competitors—Hynix and Samsung—who had spent billions on similar licenses. As Appleton has described this multifaceted strategic coup, "We ended up with about $3 or $4 billion worth of assets, and all it cost us was [$950 million] in stock."

Appleton's legendary lightning struck again in April 2002. He took advantage of the recession-battered Toshiba to buy a DRAM operation valued at about $2 billion for only $300 million. The purchase also eliminated a key rival in the market and helped allow pricing to return to profitability. In a celebration of this well-timed tactic, Appleton noted, "This transaction clearly demonstrates Micron's commitment to further strengthen its memory business in the face of a significant industry downturn."

▀▀■ When Ruthless Patience Trumps Irrational Impetuousness

> ■ Fair Isaac's "tiger" patiently stalks its HNC Software prey over three long years and finally consummates a "dream acquisition" immediately accretive to earnings.

So far, we have seen companies such as Nortel and Exodus exhibit a very costly "irrational impetuousness" in the execution of their acquisition strategies. We have also seen other companies such as IDT and Micron opportunistically swoop in to pick up strategic assets for a song.

With this last example, I want to underscore that one of the most important qualities of the well-timed acquisition strategy is not just the "opportunistic swoop." Rather, it is that antonym of irrational impetuousness: ruthless patience.

Fair Isaac's Acquisitive Tiger Waits Patiently at the Watering Hole

> *"The tiger does not hunt out in the open like the lion. It waits patiently in the long grass, perhaps near to the water's edge ... When the prey comes within 20 meters, the tiger attacks."*

—The Open Door Web site

Fair Isaac is one of the leaders in so-called credit-scoring systems. These very complex, statistics-based forecasting systems are used to evaluate the risk profiles of people like you and me when we apply for credit cards, mortgages, and other kinds of loans; and Fair Isaac's customers range from major credit card companies and commercial lenders to insurers, retailers, and cable and phone companies.

In 1999, Fair Isaac and its brilliant CEO, Tom Grudnowski, began what turned out to be a three-year hunt for HNC software. HNC had been spun off from the U.S. Department of Defense in 1986. The company owned a patented form of "predictive technology" that could be applied to forecast human behavior across a broad range of activities and applications. Accordingly, HNC offered obvious strategic synergies for Fair Isaac's run up the analytical software growth path.

After its first look at HNC in 1999, Grudnowski and his executive team concluded that HNC—along with much of the stock market—was considerably overvalued. However, later that year, HNC spun off one of its own business units called Retek. This dropped HNC's valuation as a standalone company down toward a more reasonable level.

At this point, Fair Isaac took a second look. Again, however, it demurred—still convinced that at HNC's rich stock price—

symptomatic of a broader tech bubble—the acquisition would not be accretive to earnings, no matter how strategically attractive it seemed.

Finally, after the tech bubble burst—and after a prolonged slump in HNC's stock price—came the third look at HNC. At this point, the patient Fair Isaac "tiger" acquired its HNC prey in 2002. Moreover, it did so at a huge discount relative to the original 1999 asking price. Analyst Kevin Richardson waxed eloquently about the deal:

> It's like a dream acquisition ... It's been a long time that people have talked about how good these two companies fit together ... Although they have many of the same customers ... the combined company could offer soup-to-nuts services, as well as gain access to new markets.

In fact, in just one year after Fair Isaac finally brought HNC into its fold, revenue jumped 60 percent—from $392 million to $629 million. More significantly, net income per share more than quadrupled—from $0.48 per share to $2.12. This was a "dream acquisition" indeed—one highly accretive to earnings precisely because it was so well timed.

Key Points

- **Acquisitions and Divestitures**
  - Companies acquire other companies for many different strategic reasons. The acquisition target might open new markets or own a complementary new technology, be a crucial link in the supply chain, or possess a key patent. Or the target might just be a key rival that needs to be eliminated if prices are to be raised.
  - Whereas the dictates of corporate strategy tell us the "why" of an acquisition, it is the Master Cyclist who understands the importance of timing in the tactical implementation of that strategy.
- **The "Buy High, Sell Low" Reactive Cyclist Blues**
  - Reactive Cyclists, intoxicated by the bullish fumes of a late-stage expansion, often turn the "buy low, sell high" rule completely on its head. However, overpriced acquisitions saddle a company with a long-term competitive cost disadvantage.
  - Reactive Cyclists that debt-finance their acquisitions at a time in the interest rate cycle when interest rates are high run the risk of a major cash flow problem—and possible bankruptcy—when a recession hits and revenues fall.
- **Buying Low and Selling High—or Just Sitting It Out!**
  - The Master Cyclist never impulsively make an acquisition if the stock price is too high—no matter how compelling the strategic reason.
  - The acquisitive Master Cyclist uses a highly sophisticated understanding of the business cycle— and related stock market and interest rate cycles— to tactically time any key strategic acquisition or divestiture.

CHAPTER

The Art of "Cherry Picking" and Other Well-Timed Tactics of the Human Resources Manager

Production and Inventory Control

Human Resources Management

Marketing and Pricing

Acquisitions and Divestitures

Risk Management

Capital Expenditures

"Take away my people but leave my factories, and soon grass will grow on factory floors. Take away my factories but leave my people, and soon we will have a new and better factory."

—Andrew Carnegie

Most clichés become clichés because they embody an inevitable and inalienable truth. So it is with the business cliché that "people are our most important assets." It's too bad that so many Reactive Cyclist companies unwittingly abuse these assets due to their failure to understand the business cycle and how human resources should be strategically and tactically deployed over the course of that cycle.

To understand the full extent of this problem, consider this profile of the typical Reactive Cyclist executive team: Despite Fed rate hikes, rising oil prices, an inverting of the yield curve, and other warnings of a possible recession (as discussed more fully in Chapter 11, "The Master Cyclist's Favorite Forecasting Tools"), the team continues to hire new workers well into the late, last-gasp stages of an economic expansion. Moreover, it often does so at the kind of premium wages that must be paid in a very tight labor market.

Of course, when the recession hits, the Reactive Cyclist then has to fire, or lay off, a large portion of the workforce. The resultant drop in morale causes the company's best and most mobile workers to begin looking elsewhere for a job—not only because of fear that the ax will fall next on their neck but also because they know that with the loss of good employees, their job just got that much harder. The end result: Along with the least wanted workers being laid off, the company loses some of its best employees to more enlightened rivals.

The problems do not stop here, however. Traumatized by the downturn and now wary of ever going on another hiring binge again, the Reactive Cyclist remains out of the labor market *even after the recession has bottomed and the economy is flashing new signals of a likely recovery*. While its rivals begin hiring some of the best talent at bargain wages, the Reactive Cyclist team remains flat on its heels. In the end, the company—and its shareholders!—get hit on both sides of the head because it does not have the richest talent base to maintain its competitive advantage.

As you will now see, a number of very well-timed HR strategies and tactics can be deployed by the business cycle-sensitive executive team to escape this Reactive Cyclist trap.

▰▰ ■ "Cherry Picking" the Talent Pool in Anticipation of Recovery

- ■ Avon loves a "persistently rotten economy" because it creates an ever-larger pool of recruits to sell its cosmetics to women who cannot afford the more-expensive department store creams when times are tough.

- ▦ Progressive Insurance robs not the cradle but rather the college campuses during recessions to sign up and train high-quality college recruits desperate for jobs.

- ■ Isis Pharmaceuticals leverages a sharp downturn in the biotech industry to lock top scientist talent into permanent long-term positions at bargain salaries.

- ▦ A "Lone Ranger" Lehman Brothers goes contrarianly against the industry grain to stock up on elite stock brokerage talent laid off by recession-battered competitors—and positions itself beautifully for the next bull market.

"Countercyclical hiring may ... provide a company with a competitive advantage. By engaging in bargain hunting during downturns and hiring talent that would probably not be available during upturns, a company may gain a critical edge over its competitors."

—Professors Charles Greer and Timothy Ireland[1]

In the deep dark depths of a recession, the last thing that many companies want to do is to hire more people. Not so for the Master Cyclist. The Master Cyclist knows that it is precisely at the trough of a recession that the labor pool will be at its deepest and wage pressures will have subsided. That is a great time to "cherry pick" this labor market with the goal of staffing the company with the most talented workers at bargain wages.

As the preceding excerpt from Professors Greer and Ireland illustrates, by using this cherry-picking tactic, the Master Cyclist executive team gains a critical competitive advantage. This is because *it is able to deploy a more highly skilled workforce with lower labor costs than its rivals when the new expansion begins.*

Avon's Million Women March

> *"To Andrea Jung, a persistently rotten economy is a beautiful thing. Others may see falling sales, lower profits and layoffs, but Jung, the chief executive of Avon Products Inc., sees an ever larger pool of women she can recruit to sell Avon cosmetics to an equally large pool of women who cannot afford department store creams.*
>
> **—Claudia Deutsch, *International Herald Tribune***

Avon Products is the world's largest door-to-door cosmetics queen. It fields an army of almost 5 million "Avon Ladies" who directly market to the public. Besides cosmetics, the company's products range from perfumes and toiletries to clothes, jewelry, and home furnishing; and Avon boasts almost $8 billion in sales a year.

As the economy turned down in 2001, Avon's CEO, Andrea Jung, and her executive team recognized that the downturn would result in "an ever-larger pool of women" to recruit to sell its products. Moreover, the Master Cyclists at Avon also understood that in a weak economy, Avon's products would be more attractive to all those women who would not be able to "afford department store creams."

To bring this talent into the fold, Avon revitalized an old program called Sales Leadership in which the company's top performers are taught how to recruit, train, and supervise their own group of representatives. This program, coupled with a number of other equally aggressive initiatives allowed Avon to expand its workforce by almost one third—or by roughly one million people!

The results of Avon's countercyclical hiring strategy and "million women march" was nothing short of spectacular. As CEO Jung and "right-hand woman" Susan Kropf rightfully boasted in their 2002 Annual Report message to shareholders: "[I]n another year of depressed stock prices, Avon's shares rose 16 percent, outperforming competitors and the S&P 500," while sales grew by almost twice the historical average and net income increased by 20 percent.

Nor was this march up the performance scale a one-year wonder. In 2003, earnings increased by another 25 percent to a record $2.78 a share while Avon's share price increased 25 percent to an all-time high. Moreover, Avon's success carried right into 2004, with another 27 percent increase in earnings per share and a very lucky 13 percent increase in sales.

Progressive's Generals Go with a "Generalist" Strategy

"[We] hired and trained over 3,000 external new claims representatives for a net increase of over 1,500. A soft employment market afforded us high-energy adjuster trainees."

—Glenn Renwick, CEO, Progressive Insurance

The Progressive example is interesting because it illustrates how at least some more highly sophisticated companies use the occasion of a recession to transform cheap raw recruit "generalists" into a highly polished and well-trained workforce.

With more than $10 billion in sales and more than 25,000 employees, Progressive has become the third largest auto insurer in the market. It also offers a host of other insurance products for everything from motorcycles, RVs, and snowmobiles to collateral insurance for auto lenders.

In monitoring the macroeconomic environment, Progressive's very astute executive team pays very close attention to a number of economic indicators, one of the most important of which is the *unemployment rate*. At first glance, following the unemployment rate seems to be counterintuitive for a sophisticated Master Cyclist like Progressive. That is because the unemployment rate is a "lagging indicator" that has little signaling value when it comes to forecasting or anticipating recessions. That is, while other "leading economic indicators" such as housing starts and auto sales move up *before* an expansion begins in earnest and move down *before* a recession begins, by the time the unemployment rate starts to rise, the recession is usually upon us.

However, in this particular case, Progressive closely follows the unemployment rate as a central part of a human resources strategy, which entails hiring college graduate "generalists" with little or no experience in the industry and then training these "raw recruits" in the Progressive way. This strategy is particularly important for Progressive because, as a service organization, labor is one of its largest expenses.

Of course, the best time to cherry pick such talent right off the college diploma lines is when the unemployment rate is high. That is precisely what Progressive did during and immediately after the 2001 recession—as indicated by the observation of Progressive's CEO, Glen Renwick, in the excerpt beginning this example; he clearly took advantage of a "soft employment market" to add "high-quality, high-energy adjuster trainees."

Isis Pharmaceuticals Patiently Waits to Permanently Hire

"When strategies require very high-quality or highly skilled employees who cannot usually be hired during upturns, countercyclical hiring may be particularly attractive."

—Professors Charles Greer and Timothy Ireland

The particularly astute variation of Isis Pharmaceuticals on this cherry-picking theme might be the most sophisticated of all. It illustrates how a company patiently relied on short-term contract labor during an extended expansionary period when wage pressures were high and then used the occasion of an economic and industry downturn to increase hiring of permanent, highly skilled workers.

The Isis name comes from Egyptian mythology and a famous tale about Queen Isis who used her magic powers to restore the body of her husband and brother, Osiris. This company name is quite apt because Isis Pharmaceuticals seeks to use its leading-edge "antisense technology" to restore the health of people afflicted with a wide range of diseases. This leading-edge technology is used to modify RNA to inhibit cells from producing disease-causing proteins, and one of the company's top products treats cytomegalovirus retinitis, which causes blindness in AIDS patients.

During the long period of economic expansion leading up to the 2001 recession, as labor became scarce and wage pressures increased, Isis came to rely more and more on a strong presence of temporary workers and postdoctoral students who were hired with shorter-term commitments.

However, when the recession hit and conditions in the company's own industry deteriorated markedly, Isis took a very different tack. It aggressively hired from the now deep talent pool. Moreover, it hired many of the most highly skilled workers on a permanent basis at more stable market wage rates. In this way, Isis helped to ensure itself a better caliber employee, a more committed company-employee relationship, and an established talent base in preparation for economic recovery.

Lehman (Doesn't) Cut Against the Brokerage Grain

> *"In this climate of austerity, Lehman Brothers ... is bucking the trend: In an effort to reinforce its critical mass in bad times, the firm expanded its head count by more than 20 percent [through the March 2001 recession]."*
>
> —**Michael Santoli,** ***Barron's***

This final example of a cherry-picking strategy illustrates how one "Lone Ranger" contrarian went against any entire industry grain. [2] The Lone Ranger Lehman Brothers has a well-deserved reputation on Wall Street as one of the most aggressive of traders in the business. In managing more than $160 *billion* in assets, Lehman's offerings of financial services include both investment and merchant banking, underwriting, stocks and bonds, asset management, institutional sales, and, last but not least, private client services.

As the economy slide into the March 2001 recession in the wake of the bursting of the stock market bubble, most of Wall Street's brokerage houses were using a butcher knife rather than a scalpel to cut their labor costs. Indeed, even deep-pocketed giants such as Credit Suisse First Boston, Merrill Lynch, and Goldman Sachs all implemented dramatic cuts. More broadly, securities firms cut jobs by more than 30,000—almost 10 percent of the workforce. Moreover, along with these job cuts came significant pay cuts for those still standing.

Ever the contrarian, Lehman's Master Cyclists saw this industry downbeat as a propitious time to cherry pick some of the elite talent falling by the recessionary wayside—while positioning the company for a strong presence in the equity markets come the rebound.

Of course, it vastly helped Lehman in terms of providing the cash flow and resources needed for such a gambit that during this period of strategic expansion, the bond market—one of Lehman's traditional strengths—was very strong. So it was that as the pink slips flew at other companies, Lehman was in the enviable position of having a large labor market from which to choose.

Not only was the company able to hire some of the best laid-off talent from its rivals. Taking a page out of Progressive's book, it also scooped up some of the crème de la crème of the latest MBA and college graduating crops.

Of course, in the soft labor market, Lehman's newly acquired talent came at a significant discount. This gave Lehman a future cost advantage over more-burdened rivals. In this way, Lehman CEO, Richard Fuld, could explicitly "challenge the company's bigger rivals for business when better times return."

▀▀ ■ Protecting Your Workforce During Recessions

■ Programmable chip wizard Xilinx preserves its highly skilled workforce during a recession using creative measures such as sabbatical leaves, tiered pay cuts, and forced vacations.

"After big workforce cuts, the surviving employees become overburdened, make more mistakes and accomplish less. As morale and productivity slips, so will profits. The [Trends Research Institute] refers to the downsizing trend as 'dumbsizing.'"

—*The Post-Standard*, Syracuse, New York

Nothing can kill employee morale faster than massive layoffs during a recession. That is why at the first hint of a possible recession, the Master Cyclist executive team begins to deploy any one of a number of defensive tactics designed to humanely "right size" the company by the time the recession hits—while at the same time maintaining employee morale.

The first and most obvious tactic is just to stop hiring—and perhaps supplement the workforce as need be with more temporary hires. This effectively begins the process of reducing the permanent workforce because normal attrition will begin to take hold. It also reduces what can be a potentially heavy labor cost burden when new permanent workers are hired at premium prices—and then must be let go with lucrative severance packages just months later.

A second more subtle response, perhaps necessary if the recessionary signals are particularly strong, is to implement an early-retirement program to accelerate the rate of attrition. This likewise can prove particularly effective in managing labor costs because older workers also tend to be more expensive workers.

Still a third type of response as the recession takes hold is to offer employees financial inducements to take education "sabbaticals" or other forms of leave—and thereby cut costs while preserving the employment relationship. This is a tactic you will see put to exceedingly good use by the computer chipmaker Xilinx.

Xilinx Zealously Protects Its Intellectual Capital

*"Companies should realize that their most talented workers
are the most marketable and could be in high demand
once the economy picks up. That's why they should let them
know they are valued and discuss their roles in the future
of the organization."*

—Susan Gebelein, Personnel Decisions International

Xilinx is one of the leading suppliers of so-called field-programmable gate arrays. Such programmable chips can be used by engineers quite literally out in the field who are seeking to design specialized integrated circuits. These circuits can then later be produced in large quantities for distribution to computer manufacturers and other users in industries ranging from aerospace and industrial control to networking and telecommunications.

Leading up to the 2001 recession—and like many high-flying but business cycle-illiterate tech companies—Xilinx's executive team failed to pay proper attention to the macroeconomic danger signs. As a result, the company consistently overestimated its revenues and wound up missing its forecasts four quarters in a row in 2001.

Fortunately, Xilinx's executive team did not panic as the recession took hold. Instead, the company and its CEO, Wim Roelandts, responded *not* with layoffs per se but rather with a highly sophisticated tactical gambit designed to both cut costs and save the company's valuable intellectual capital—its so-called knowledge workers.

With this tactical gambit, Xilinx offered its employees a year-long sabbatical program that paid them a small stipend if they went to school or worked for a nonprofit. In addition, Xilinx adopted a system of tiered pay cuts and, where necessary, forced vacations.

Underlying these programs was the knowledge that the cost of losing, and later replacing, a trained engineer runs about a quarter of million dollars. Therefore, Xilinx was understandably reluctant just to lay off people to shore up its bottom line because it knew that as soon as the recovery was on the way, any of the so-called labor savings would be obliterated by the hiring and retraining process.

This tactical gambit not only saved Xilinx the cost of search and training costs of new hiring. It also prevented its competitors from hiring these workers, picking their brains, and then effectively stealing some of Xilinx's best ideas and processes!

Perhaps best of all, under this protective tactical HR umbrella, Xilinx employees maintained high morale throughout the recession and were much better able to focus solely on product innovation without the distraction and stress of losing any of their teammates or even losing their own job.

Ultimately, Xilinx's tactical HR gambit had a very lucrative payoff. Not only did it save Xilinx more than $35 million in labor costs. As the economy and chip sector began to recover in 2002, Xilinx was able to offer a suite of innovative new products in each of its three major product categories. These new products quickly allowed Xilinx to begin grabbing market share from other competitors whose product development had been slowed and substantially degraded through layoffs. The result was a solidification of Xilinx's position as one of the leading providers of logic devices.

Most broadly, the Xilinx team seems to have learned an important lesson from its recessionary travails. In the wake of that recession, CFO Kris Chellam created a task force to develop software that injects more business cycle indicators into company forecasts. The new system not only ties point of sale from distributors to in-house marketing and inventory data. It also tracks capital spending by the telecom industry and the profit performance of the S&P 500. This approach helps Xilinx determine whether its customers have enough cash flow to invest heavily in its products.

Making "No-Layoffs" Policies Work the Master Cyclist Way

> ■ Nucor Steel uses wage and work-hour flexibility, tactical cross-training, and a highly supportive organizational culture to make its "no-layoffs" policy a strong asset rather than recession liability.

"Drowned out by the layoff headlines is the heartening news that a few companies still offer job security. What's more, although the recession has reduced their number, many in the no-layoff club are tops in their respective industries: Nucor is the nation's most profitable steelmaker. Southwest Airlines, which hasn't had a layoff in its 31-year history, is the most consistently profitable airline. The duck commercials are generating record sales at insurer AFLAC, which has had no layoffs in its 47 years."

—*U.S. News & World Report*

Every company that adopts a "no-layoffs" policy implicitly acknowledges a fundamental economic tradeoff between the cost savings from workforce reductions during recessions and the often greater costs of rehiring and retraining during expansions. As Xilinx's executive team clearly understood, this tradeoff is particularly important in higher-skilled occupations such as engineering and design where training costs are high.

Avoiding such higher costs is not the only reason that some companies opt for a no-layoffs strategy. A second is that companies often bundle the promise of "no layoffs" with higher wages and benefits to become "employers of choice." This is a highly coveted status that often allows companies to attract the very best workers while enjoying the cost-saving benefits of very high retention rates.

Finally, as a third checkmark in the plus column, no layoffs help keep employee morale high, with morale being an important intangible asset that helps boost productivity.

Despite these benefits, companies that adopt "no-layoff" policies will not always be more successful than other companies who fire and hire with the business cycle seasons. Rather, as one of the key findings of this book, the real long-term success of any no layoffs policy comes *only if* the executive team has also successfully applied a set of collateral tools and tactics to help buffer the company and its workforce from recessionary risk.

The Nucor Steel example illustrates just such a situation. Here we will see one particularly astute Master Cyclist company—in a highly cyclical industry!—that has relied upon a system of wage and work-hour flexibility, tactical cross-training, and a highly supportive organizational culture to keep *both* its shareholders *and* employees happy over all phases of the business cycle.

Nucor Shares the Pain for Gain

> *"Keep coming in good times, even seven days a week and stash some of the money away, because we can guarantee the good times won't last."*

> **—Jim Coblin, vice president of human resources, Nucor**

With more than $6 billion in annual sales and roughly 10,000 employees, Nucor offers its customers both hot- and cold-rolled steel, steel fasteners, and even metal buildings. The company, which relies heavily on the recycling of scrap metal, also is the largest U.S. producer of steel joists and girders.

That Nucor's executive team is highly attentive to the business cycle is a very good thing because the steel industry is one of the most highly cyclical of industries. This cyclicity is a function of the fact that many of the steel industry's largest customers are in cyclical industries themselves. These include autos, construction, and consumer appliances—all of which are highly interest rate sensitive as well as sensitive to the vagaries of consumer and investor confidence that can flag in the days and months leading up to recessions.

Much of Nucor's business cycle management success can be traced to its very skillful management of its human resources. Nucor's most important HR tools and tactics include the following:

- A highly flexible "Share the Pain" program that allows the company to taper its labor costs in recessions without loss of productive capacity.
- A highly flexible and "cross-trained" workforce that can be shifted to other functions as needed.
- And, perhaps most important, a highly supportive organizational culture that breeds a fierce loyalty among employees and a uncommon willingness in today's times to sacrifice for the company when times are tough.

Under Share the Pain, both work hours and wages are highly flexible. For example, the annual bonuses for line personnel and foremen range from 80 percent to 150 percent of base pay, depending on conditions. Moreover, slowdowns can also result in both reduced wages—as much as 20 percent—as well as hours worked. In addition, Nucor has adopted a "progressive scale" for sharing the pain, whereby department heads and top managers share proportionally *more* pain as conditions warrant.

For example, for department heads, slowdowns can result in a reduction of up to one third or more of pay. In contrast, top managers' pay, which is based on the company's return on equity, might be cut by as much as two thirds or even three fourths. This approach proves particularly effective at building loyalty and morale in the lower ranks—and staving off any and all attempts by union organizers to bring Nucor into their fold.

As a further consideration to its workers, Nucor's executive team does not just slow everyone and everything down during recessions. In slow times, many of Nucor's cross-trained employees are moved off the production line and given everything from brooms to tools to help refurbish facilities and repair equipment. In this vein, Nucor also tactically accelerates any of its modernization and routine maintenance efforts during downturns.

The beauty of Nucor's approach is that labor costs are cut in response to slowdowns in demand—without the company losing any of its production capacity or workers. Because of this flexibility—facilitated as it is by a highly supportive organizational culture—Nucor can ramp up quickly to meet increased demand and can closely match costs to monthly changes in demand.

▰▰▰ The (Not-So-) Well-Timed Contract Negotiation

> ▰ United Airlines brings down an entire fleet of "legacy carriers" with a "gold-standard" labor contract foolishly signed in the white-hot heat of an economic expansion.

As a final cautionary note on the art of Master Cyclist human resources management, it is useful to warn of the dangers of negotiating long-term labor contracts in the late stages of an economic expansion. Typically, in this stage of the business cycle, the unemployment rate is very low, wage demands are high, unions have maximum bargaining power, and companies are enjoying robust profits—which labor negotiators will be eyeing hungrily. The example of United Airlines shows that entering into an overly expensive long-term labor contract at the wrong time can be hazardous not just to a company's health but also to any industry where "pattern bargaining" is the norm.

United Signs on the Dotted Line of Doom

"The shock wave from the United contract is still reverberating through the airline industry nearly a year after the carrier's management ... offered hefty pay raises and substantial concessions on work rules.

"Because each airline closely watches rivals, the United contract caused management groups industrywide to swallow hard and pilot unions to reassess their demands. It set a new gold standard for pilot compensation at the large network carriers..."

—*Dallas Morning News*

In the summer of 2000, in the white-hot climax of the longest economic expansion in U.S. history and after many months of bitter negotiations in which its pilots refused to fly overtime, the United Airlines executive team completely capitulated to union demands. It agreed to a contract that resulted in an immediate increase in pilot wages of 21 to 28 percent plus a 4 percent increase per year thereafter.

The contract not only solidified the dubious position of United Airlines as the carrier paying the highest labor costs in the airline industry. This contract was also met with howls of protest by other so-called legacy carriers such as American and Delta in an industry where "pattern bargaining" for the unionized legacy carriers is prevalent. In this particular case, as the preceding excerpt indicates, the pattern set in the United contract was "a new gold standard for pilot compensation."

Multiple ironies are associated with what happened in the aftermath of this severe Reactive Cyclist stumble by United's executive team. Not only did the burden of these high wages help drive the company into bankruptcy in the aftermath of the 9/11 terrorist shock to the industry. Those United pilots, who just three years earlier had popped the champagne corks to celebrate their good fortune, found themselves forced to endure not only huge wage cuts and increases in hours worked but also the virtual decimation of their once seemingly secure pensions. As the final insult, the dramatic rise in the wage structures of the legacy carriers provided a competitive opening big enough for new low-cost upstarts such as Jet Blue to fly an Airbus through.

Few better examples of "be careful, you might get what you ask for" exist. However, the real villain in the piece is not the "greedy pilots" so much as the foolish band of United executives who picked the absolute worse time in the business cycle to run up the contract negotiations white flag.

■■■ Key Points

■ **Human Resources Management**
- The Reactive Cyclist continues to hire at premium wages into the late stages of an economic expansion and then engages in massive layoffs when the recession hits. This "morale buster" leads to a further exodus of some of the company's best workers.
- The Master Cyclist deploys a wide range of tools and tactics to escape this Reactive Cyclist trap.

■ **"Cherry Picking" the Talent Pool in Anticipation of Recovery**
- At the recessionary trough, the labor pool will be deepest and wage pressures least. That is a great time to hire the most talented workers at bargain wages.
- By such "cherry picking," the Master Cyclist gains a competitive advantage by deploying a more highly skilled workforce with lower labor costs than rivals.

- **Protecting and Preserving the Workforce During Recessions**
  - Both attrition and early retirement programs can be used to humanely "right size" a company in anticipation of a recession.
  - Sabbatical leaves, tiered pay cuts, forced vacations, and other creative options can help protect your highly skilled workforce in a downturn and prevent poaching rivals from "stealing" your employees and company secrets.
- **Making "No-Layoffs" Policies Work**
  - No-layoffs policies can keep morale high and boost productivity.
  - Companies that bundle a no-layoffs policy with higher wages and benefits often also become "employers of choice." This allows them to attract the best workers and enjoy cost-saving high retention rates.
  - However, the real long-term success of any no-layoffs policy comes *only if* the executive team has also successfully applied a set of collateral tools and tactics to help buffer the company and its workforce from the ravages of the business cycle.
- **The (Not-So-) Well-Timed Contract Negotiation**
  - Never negotiate a long-term contract in the heat of an economic expansion when the labor market is at its tightest and wage pressures are highest.

CHAPTER

5

"Macromanaging" Your Production, Inventory, and Supply Chain

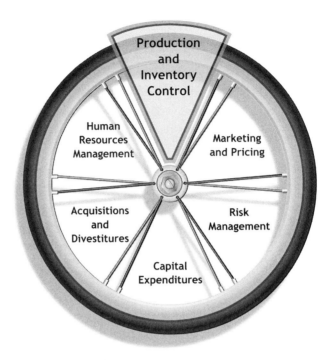

"This year is shaping up to have the roughest truck-market conditions in at least seven years, and perhaps since the inflation of the late 1970s and early 1980s. Through it all, Paccar is expected to remain in the black. Every year since 1939, it has trudged through war, inflation, high interest rates and oil crises to churn out profit..."

—Luke Timmerman, *Seattle Times*

Companies that continue to increase their production and build up inventories as a recession approaches inevitably suffer in myriad ways. Most obviously, bloated inventories increase holding costs, leave a company more vulnerable to breakage and pilferage, and, in the worst-case scenario, result in costly inventory write-downs. More subtly, a large inventory overhang can also leave a company with obsolete or out-of-fashion products that then must be dumped at fire-sale prices.

Bloating the inventory as a recession approaches is not, however, the only—or perhaps even the worst—sin of the Reactive Cyclist. Indeed, *companies that fail to increase production and build inventories in anticipation of an economic recovery are often left at the starting gate by far more nimble rivals.* The result, often, is a sudden loss of market share to more business cycle-sensitive competitors able to offer the latest products and styles in far more abundance as the economy kicks once again into high gear.

In this chapter, I review some of the major "do's" and "don'ts" of business cycle-sensitive production and inventory control. Perhaps even more important, I also introduce you to the critical difference between the "old-school" *micromanagement* of one's supply chain and a leading-edge *macromanagement* approach more in tune with today's global environment.

▪▪ The "Don'ts" of Production and Inventory Control

- ▪ Cisco's executive team rejects the use of macroeconomic forecasting and falls prey to a classic "bullwhip effect."
- ▪ Chipmaker Conexant highlights the disastrous consequences of top management ignoring internal company data and gunning the production engine in the face of declining demand.
- ▪ Electronics manufacturer Nu Horizons underscores how key industry-specific indicators can help an executive team safely navigate past recessionary shoals—but only if the CEO heeds its signals.

Reactive Cyclist executive teams are prone to at least two types of errors when it comes to managing their production and inventory levels over the course of the business cycle. The first, and most obvious, is that a company's executive team might fail to build either an internal or external forecasting capability and therefore has no way to anticipate movements in the business cycle.

The second, and perhaps even less-forgivable sin, is that some companies actually have the relevant forecasting information in-house to make the right decisions! However, because of either the business cycle illiteracy of the top management or various structural impediments in the organization to getting the information to the right decision makers, the company chooses to ignore that information.

Cisco Gets Whipped by the Bullwhip Effect

"People see a shortage and intuitively they forecast higher. Salespeople don't want to be caught without supply, so they make sure they have supply by forecasting more sales than they expect. Procurement needs 100 of a part, but they know if they ask for 100, they'll get 80. So they ask for 120 to get 100."

—Forio Business Solutions

What Forio has just done is illustrate the classic "bullwhip effect" problem in operations management. This is precisely the problem that befell Cisco when it spectacularly bungled its production and inventory control in the months leading up to the 2001 recession.

This bullwhip effect describes a situation in which so-called *shortage gaming* and a collateral *phantom demand* are likely to lead to levels of production and inventory far in excess of the underlying real demand for a product. To see more clearly how this bullwhip effect works, consider that in the middle of the 1990s expansion and at the height of the tech boom, Cisco had terrible trouble filling its orders fast enough. These chronic shortages in the market, in turn, created a frenzied situation in which customers would *back order much more product than they actually needed* in the hopes they would get a big enough allotment to fill their actual demand. (For example, they might order two routers hoping to get one.)

The result, over time, was that even as Cisco was able to catch up to its *real* demand, it kept trying to increase production and inventories to meet the ever-growing *phantom* demand. CEO John Chambers later admitted to the *Economist* magazine: "We never built models to anticipate something of this magnitude."

Now here's the punch line: If Cisco's executive team had not explicitly rejected the use of macroeconomics indicators in its business-forecasting model, it would have been better able to see the 2001 recession coming and, more important, distinguish between an ever-growing phantom demand and a suddenly shrinking real demand. However, because of the company's lack of business cycle literacy, Cisco was left holding a very big multi-billion-dollar bag of inventory write-downs.

Conexant's Generals Ignore Some Specific Recessionary Data

> *"Communications chip suppliers, smarting from the double indignity of quarterly revenue declines and bloated inventories, last week began the healing process by accepting their lot and moving on. ... Conexant Systems Inc., Newport Beach, Calif., took a pretax charge of $148.6 million for inventory reserves in its fiscal 2001 second quarter and posted negative gross margins as production costs exceeded sales."*
>
> **—Electric Supplies and Manufacturing Online**

The rags-to-riches-back-to-ragged Conexant flew like a meteor through the Internet bubble skies—only to fall on the sword of its own hubris. Spun off by the defense company Rockwell in January 1999, the company had sales that rocketed up to more than $2 billion by the year 2000—a truly astonishing burst.

During this time, Conexant's stock price increased more than sixfold. However, by the end of 2002, the company had devolved into an embarrassing "penny stock" forced to divest many of its assets.

Conexant's executive team empathetically did not make the same mistake as Cisco's and totally ignore the increasingly urgent signals of recession emanating from the economy. Instead, in a supreme irony, *Conexant's supremely overconfident top execs simply ignored readily available company data indicating dramatically falling chip demand.*

Indeed, within Conexant's own supply chain management "shop," analysts saw quite clearly that inventories at the company's distributor locations and in Taiwan were going up, that wafer supplies were becoming plentiful in Asia as capacity factors were going down, and that customers were no longer complaining if an order was shipped a few days late. These internal indicators all showed that the business and chip cycles were showing signs of turning down.

When combined with the external indicators of a falling stock market, an oil price shock, and a flattening yield curve, Conexant's own internal data should have been a strong clue for its top management to take a hard, fresh look at its business situation. Instead, it was damn the recessionary torpedoes and full speed ahead.

The vehicle for this hubris was a rose-colored demand forecast that flew recklessly on the wings of hope and past performance while flying in the face of the reality of their very own real data. On the basis of this wildly overoptimistic forecast, production plans were dutifully made, raw materials were dutifully purchased, and, worst of all, Conexant entered into "take or pay" long-term contracts that locked them into overly optimistic production levels so that they could meet forecast volumes.

The outcome was predictable. As the bottom fell out of the semiconductor market in late 2000, revenue performance dropped dramatically. In the (bitter) penny-stock end, Conexant wound up recording almost a *billion* dollars in inventory write-downs and other special charges over the next two years.

Perhaps the most incredible thing about this abysmal performance is the happy, blameless face that the company's CEO, Dwight Decker, tried to put on this titanic disaster. As the lead off to the

2001 Annual Report—a year in which his company lost almost $1.5 billion and shareholders lost more than $1 billion in equity— Decker had this to say:

> *Conexant strengthened product portfolios and market positions throughout fiscal 2001 while carefully managing cash and expenditures during the deepest, most abrupt business reversal in the history of the semiconductor industry.*

Forgive me, but there was absolutely nothing that was careful about how Conexant managed its way through a recession that was very well signaled and anything but "abrupt."

Nu Horizons Discounts an All-Important Industry Indicator

> *"We agree that there has been some recent weakness in book-to-bill ratios, but we continue to believe that it is a short-term correction."*

—Arthur Nadata, president and CEO, Nu Horizons

The Canadian-based Nu Horizons is a leading global distributor of a wide range of high technology components—from clock and timing devices, computer products, and microcontrollers to flat panel display solutions, microprocessors, and the odd-sounding but revolutionary "opto" electronics. This is a company that didn't ignore its own internal recessionary forecasts like Conexant. However, its CEO did heavily discount a very important leading economic indicator for the company's industry—so-called book-to-bill ratios.

Book-to-bill ratios compare the total dollars of product that are shipped to customers in a given month to the bookings in the same month for future deliveries; and any reading above one signals that orders are outpacing deliveries and signifies a healthy demand for product. Once this ratio dips below one, it indicates that inventories might be building faster than demand is growing. That's a clear warning sign of possible trouble ahead.

As the preceding excerpt from Nu Horizons CEO Arthur Nadata indicates, he clearly did not heed this signal. Rather, he saw the softening of the industry's book-to-bill ratios as signaling merely a "short-term correction." In Nadata's defense, one might argue that the company's executive team simply had a legitimate disagreement with the data.

To be frank, that argument simply does not wash. When Nadata's industry-level data is viewed more properly within a broader macroeconomic context, his assertion seems more like ostrich-like behavior in the last gasp of an economic expansion rather than a well-calculated contrarian gambit. After all, a whole slew of other and broader "corroborating" economic indicators strongly signaled a faltering business cycle expansion—from rising oil prices and relentless Fed rate hikes to a collapsing stock market and an inverted yield curve.

The failure of Nu Horizons to heed those signals and continue to build up its inventory into the teeth of a recession helped lead the company to two of its worst years in its history. As its sales dropped by more than half, inventories piled up to record levels. The company's shareholders took the predictable beating as the company's stock price also fell by more than half.

■■ ■ Micromanaging—and Macromanaging!—Your Inventory

- Walgreens' *micro*management demons dance supply chain management circles around CVS.
- The superior inventory *macro*managers of trucking giant Paccar leave lumbering rival Navistar in the recessionary dust.

"Inventory turns are all about cash. ... The faster you turn your inventory, the more cash you can generate out of business, [and] the more you can invest."

—Dennis Miller, CFO, Eckerd Drugs

The sharp contrast between two drug retailing behemoths—CVS and Walgreens—and two trucking giants—Paccar and Navistar—provides an interesting illustration of the subtle but critical difference between *micromanaging* versus *macromanaging* one's inventory turnover ratio over the course of the business cycle.

In this regard, a standard piece of supply chain micromanagement advice is to "keep your inventory turnover ratio as high as possible."[1] The faster inventory turns, the lower the holding costs, and the better your cash flow. This implies that, when a business becomes totally efficient at managing its inventory turnover, the ratio will be an invariant *horizontal* line over the course of the business cycle.

The equally standard prescription to achieve this high turnover ratio involves applying a variety of "micromanagement" tools *independent* of the business cycle—from warehouse operations consolidations and improving supply chain relations to applying computer simulation models and the latest scanning technologies.

Note, however, that it is arguably as important from a Master Cyclist perspective, to *macromanage* your inventory turnover ratio. As a practical matter, this means tactically *increasing* the ratio by cutting production and trimming inventories when your forecasting models or economic indicators signal possible recession. Such a defensive retrenchment will maximize cash flow at a time when it is most likely to be needed.

More subtly, when economic indicators begin signaling a new expansion, it might prove tactically sensible for a company to actually *drive down* the inventory turnover ratio by building up inventories! In this way, your company will be better positioned than rivals to offer the broadest range of the latest products as the economy roars back to life.

These dynamics suggest that the conventional measure of a uniformly high and horizontal line for the turnover ratio over all phases of the business cycle does not offer the best metric of superior performance. Rather, ideally, *the turnover ratio should move in a wave-like pattern* over the course of the business cycle, rising as a recession approaches and falling as the promise of a new expansion looms.

Walgreens Goes to the Head of the Micromanagement Class

"They [Walgreens] invented the centralized pharmacy system."

—**Ken Petersen, CEO, Eckerd Drugs**

CVS has more drugstores—more than 5,000 nationwide. Walgreens often generates more revenue—around $40 *billion* per year. Whichever way you want to count it, these two companies can claim the number one and number two positions in the high stakes world of drug retailing.

As a practical matter, drug retailing is a "noncyclical" sector with far less exposure to business cycle risk than highly cyclical sectors such as chemicals, semiconductors, and trucking. That is why it is a good sector to demonstrate the virtues of inventory and supply chain *micro*management *independent* of the business cycle.

In fact, Walgreens is an absolute demon when it comes to micromanaging its inventories and supply chain. As early as 1992, Walgreens adopted point-of-sale bar code scanning with sophisticated links to a "Strategic Inventory Management System." It boasts a highly efficient set of distribution centers. It quickly embraced various digital technologies such as a digital-imaging software that can spot mistakes when trucks are loaded, and, as testimony to its hegemony in the centralized pharmacy kingdom, any one of its customers can go into any Walgreens anywhere in the country and call up his or her prescription for fulfillment. By contrast, rival CVS has lagged far behind in the micromanagement game—seemingly always forced to play technological catch-up to the ever-fleet-of-foot Walgreens.

Figure 5-1 illustrates the critical difference between micromanaging and macromanaging one's production and inventory using the examples of Walgreens versus CVS (micromanagement) and two big-rig manufacturers, Paccar versus Navistar. For now, however, let's just focus on the top of Figure 5-1. It contrasts the inventory turnover ratios of Walgreens versus CVS over the five-year interval going in to and out of the 2001 recession—a period in which the economy moved from expansion to recession and back to expansion.

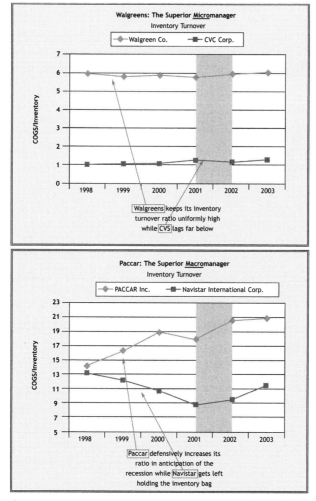

▲ **FIGURE 5-1** *Micromanaging vs. macromanaging your inventory turnover.*

Note that for both drugstore chains, very little variation in inventory turnover occurs over the course of the business cycle. The lines are roughly horizontal or flat—just as the standard micromanagement view of inventory control implies—whereas the gray area in the figure encompasses the recessionary period.

In fact, this is exactly the kind of "flat-line" pattern you would expect from two companies in a decidedly noncyclical industry sector such as drugs or food. In such noncyclical sectors, the demand for products varies little over the business cycle. After all, people still get sick and need medicine and still have to eat during recessions.

In evaluating these two companies using the standard micromanagement yardstick of highest inventory turnover ratio, *you clearly can see that Walgreen's is the superior performer.* Its ratio soars well above that of CVS over the *entire* interval—from expansion to recession and back to expansion.

From a Master Cyclist perspective, however, *this is a far too static view of the inventory management problem*—a point that, as I now explain, will soon be obvious when we examine more closely the bottom of Figure 5-1, which compares Paccar's superior *macromanagement* of inventory turnover to that of Navistar.

A More Nimble Paccar Beats Navistar to the Inventory Punch

"Big rigs are designed to take punishment from the elements of Mother Nature and the road, but every few years they take a beating from the economy."

—Luke Timmerman, *Seattle Times*

"PACCAR has established a consistent record of earnings through all phases of the economic cycle, achieving annual profits for 65 consecutive years and paying a dividend since 1941."

—Mark Pigott, CEO, PACCAR 2003 Annual Report

Paccar and Navistar both make heavy big-rig trucks, but they could not be more different in their approaches to managing the business cycle. The Master Cyclist Paccar was founded by William Pigott, Sr. in 1905, and its flagship Peterbilt and Kenworth lines remain under the control of a tightly knit family. In the past 40 years, Paccar has had only two CEOs: Charles Pigott, who assumed the reins in the mid-1960s; and his son Mark, who took over in 1997.

The hallmark of this company is an ultra-keen awareness of the business cycle, a religious following of key industry indicators such as freight tonnage, and, most of all, a nimble, accordion-like ability to ramp up or ramp down its production at the first sign of recession or recovery. As a company treasurer once put it, "We have the ability to turn off the spigot and turn it on. ... In a cyclical market, we have to have the ability to do that, and we do."

Paccar's nimbleness is deeply rooted in the company's own pragmatic culture. As one assembly line operator described it to the *Seattle Times*, "Workers appreciate how [executives] don't go into denial or stonewall when a downswing is coming. They are frank and open about cuts, and ... relations between the company and its unions seem to be good."

Moreover, from the very first new employee orientation, every worker is warned that "the truck business is cyclical and they could someday be casualties. ... They say these are the facts, and this is how it is. It helps get you mentally prepared." It is in large part because of this frankness that when the economy recovers, loyal workers typically find their way back to Paccar's factories rather than the opposition's. It is also in large part because of its Master Cyclist management approach that Paccar has one of the most incredible records of profitability in a highly cyclical industry—more than 60 straight years!

As for Navistar, it seems to inhabit an alternative universe. In fact, this is a great example of a company with good products and an admirable record of technological innovation (for example, the first smokeless diesel engine). Yet this is a public company plagued by some of the worst management ever endured by shareholders.

Navistar started out as the farm equipment manufacturer International Harvester in 1902 and added trucks to its line in 1914. After a disastrous labor strike in 1979 that nearly drove the company into bankruptcy, it changed its name to Navistar in 1986, and again changed the name of its operating company in 2000. The joke, however, is that the more Navistar changed its name, the more things remained the same.

The company has been plagued by labor strife (including a "rampage shooting" that killed five employees) and charges of racial discrimination, but one of the dumbest things the company ever did was to divest its construction equipment and farm equipment business units. The dumb part, by the way, was not dumping the companies. It was management inexplicably agreeing to be responsible for the medical and life insurance benefits liabilities of the retirees. That deal saddled the company with liabilities so large that they dwarfed the company's net worth.

These and a murderer's row of other mistakes earned the bumbling Navistar a very embarrassing "We're #1!" as the company posted the worst total return to shareholders of all publicly traded companies between 1986 and 1996. Of course, it was supposed to get better when Navistar put a new CEO in charge in 1995. In fact, in an interview with the *Financial Times*, John Horne did talk a good game, vowing in 1999 that *"This is a company which will not be swayed by the cycles as we used to be."*

Still, old Reactive Cyclist habits are hard to break, and after two blowout boom years in the trucking biz in 1998 and 1999, Horne and his complacent executive crew thought it would never end as Navistar—always two steps behind Paccar in anticipating movements in the business and industry cycles—refused to retrench in the face of rising oil prices and interest rates, a growing glut of used trucks on the market, and a rapidly softening economy.

Now let's go back to the bottom of Figure 5-1. You can vividly see how Navistar got caught in the downdraft even as the Master Cyclist Paccar played the cycle like a violin.

In particular, in the figure, Paccar is clearly driving *up* its inventory turnover ratio in anticipation of the 2001 recession—swiftly cutting production and trimming inventories. That is sophisticated Master Cyclist management. In contrast, Navistar moves much less swiftly to cut production and inventories, and as a result, its turnover ratio falls dramatically.

Now here's the punch line: At this point in the business cycle, the much more defensive Paccar has maneuvered itself into a far better cash flow position—and unlike Navistar, Paccar will maintain its profitability over the entire interval.

▒▒■ Build-to-Order and Production-to-Order Strategies

"In the struggle for survival, the fittest win out at the expense of their rivals because they succeed in adapting themselves best to their environment."

—Charles Darwin

To end this chapter, I want to focus on two members of a very interesting family of strategies that involve assembling or building a product only *after* an order is made for it.[2] As the examples of Dell and KB Home show, the beauty of such *build-to-order* and *production-to-order* systems from a Master Cyclist perspective is that they obviate the need for holding large inventories and thereby help insulate a company from business cycle fluctuations.

Dell's Pioneering Build-to-Order System Chews Up Market Share

"The business model is relatively simple. Dell takes orders over the phone and through its Web site. Though Dell assembles a computer specifically for each order, making and shipping a PC usually only takes Dell 36 hours."

—Excite.com

Using its pioneering build-to-order system, Dell has been able to reduce the days of inventory it holds on hand to an average of 4 days! The result is an inventory turnover ratio that is absolutely off the charts—more than *100* as compared to less than 30 for rivals such as Gateway and Hewlett-Packard!

Dell's build-to-order system has not just dramatically cut costs. It has also proven to be *a very powerful weapon to seize market share from rivals whenever the economy has softened or plunged into recession.*

Why is this so? It has to do with Dell's ability to exploit an extremely interesting "obsolescence edge."

Just consider what happened during the 2001 recession. At the time, virtually all of Dell's major rivals—from Gateway and Hewlett-Packard to the then still-independent Compaq—relied on a business model that involved the heavy stocking of retail outlet channels. Of course, when the recession hit, all of Dell's major rivals found themselves saddled not just with huge amounts of inventory *but also with an inventory of computers and other products that had quickly become obsolete.*

Part of this obsolescence may be attributed to the famous Moore's law, which states that "the number of *transistors* per square inch on *integrated circuits* will double every year." However, such obsolescence does not result from the ever-increasing speed of computer chips alone. Other rapidly changing components come into play as well such as physically smaller hard drives with larger storage space and advanced networking features.

Now here is the important point: Faced with large amounts of obsolete inventory, Compaq, HP, and Gateway all had to cut prices to move these less-desirable, older machines. Meanwhile, with its lean-and-mean build-to-order system, Dell could offer the very latest in computing power at comparable prices. Indeed, in some cases, it could even capture a revenue-enhancing premium!

Coupled with a strong countercyclical advertising program discussed in the next chapter, the result for Dell was an avalanche of additional market share that moved the king of build-to-order to number one in the world—even as the company maintained solid profitability.

Would Charles Darwin Live in a KB Home?

"KBnxt allows us to truly construct each home one at a time. In fact, that's why we used the singular 'Home' in our name, not 'Homes.' We really are able to give the entry-level, production home buyer a very customized experience."

—Bart Pachino, senior VP, KB Home

Formerly known as Kaufman and Broad, KB Home operates in 15 states from coast-to-coast including the fast-growing Sunbelt region in Arizona, California, the Carolinas, Colorado, Florida, Georgia, Nevada, and Texas. Through an aggressive acquisition strategy, it has become one of the largest home builders in America. Building for first-time, move-up, and active adult buyers, the homes of KB Home range in size from a little less than 1,000 square feet to over 7,000 square feet, with an average price of several hundred thousand dollars.

KB Home offers an excellent example of an organization that transformed itself from a Reactive Cyclist into a superb Master Cyclist. When the worst recession since the Great Depression hit the housing market back in July 1990, KB home was caught totally by surprise with a mountain of inventory on its hands and few buyers in what had just months earlier been a red-hot housing market. KB Home dodged the bankruptcy bullet that hit many of its developer competitors, and the company's top management learned from its traumatic business cycle experience and quickly began to prepare for what they viewed as the inevitable recessionary "next time."

One important form of this Darwinian adaptation involved the more formal use of regional forecasting and market survey tools. As housing market analyst William Walter observed, "Ten years ago, KB Home might have chosen to develop houses in a particular area simply because a local executive had a 'gut feeling' that the area would appeal to people. Today, KB Home chooses to build in a particular area only after it has conducted extensive market surveys and statistical studies of the region."

Arguably, however, the even more important step KB Home's executive team took was to change the way that the company made its inventory and production decisions. In particular, following the 1990-1991 recession, KB home adopted its *production-to-order* system for preselling homes called KBnxt. Like Dell—but with a much more complicated product with greater lead times—KB Home would henceforth not begin construction on a home until a contract existed with a buyer.

This strategic shift greatly minimizes the company's risk exposure at the same time that it enhances the predictability and sustainability of its results. The approach also dovetails in an elegant way with a marketing strategy aimed at turning the stock production home into a more personalized experience. As the opening excerpt to this example indicates, by "building to suit," the company has been able to give customers exactly what they want.

■■■ Key Points

- **The "Do's" and "Don'ts" of Production and Inventory Control**
    - Reactive Cyclist executive teams that fail to *decrease* their production as a recession approaches inevitably are left with bloated inventories and obsolete or out-of-fashion products that must be dumped at fire-sale prices or written off.
    - Reactive Cyclists that fail to *increase* their production and build inventories in anticipation of an economic recovery often lose market share to more nimble rivals.

- Reactive Cyclists companies that fail to build either an internal or external forecasting capability are particularly prone to the "bullwhip effect."
- Some executive teams have the relevant forecasting information in-house, but because of leadership or organizational flaws, top executives ignore or discount the information.

Micromanaging—and Macromanaging!—Your Inventory Turnover

- Micromanaging your supply chain means keeping your inventory turnover ratio as high as possible to cut cost and improve cash flow.
- Micromanagement tools can be deployed *independent* of movements of the business cycle.
- Macromanaging your supply chain means increasing the inventory turnover ratio by cutting production and trimming inventories to maximize cash flow as a recession approaches
- Macromanaging also means allowing the inventory turnover ratio to fall through increased inventory buildups in anticipation of a new economic expansion.
- By tactically building inventories as an expansion begins, a company will be better positioned than rivals to offer the broadest range of the latest products and thereby be better able to seize market share as the economy roars back to life.

The Power of Build-to-Order and Production-to-Order Strategies

- In build- and production-to-order systems, no product is produced until an order is actually received and paid for in part or in full. Such a system obviates the need for holding large inventories and thus provides an excellent means to minimize business cycle risk.

Master Cyclist Marketing Through the Business Cycle Seasons

Production
and Inventory
Control

Human
Resources
Management

Marketing
and Pricing

Acquisitions
and
Divestitures

Risk
Management

Capital
Expenditures

"When the economic climate changes, the best retailers look for opportunity."

—Robert Tillman, CEO, Loew's

The strategic and tactical implications of Master Cyclist marketing and pricing offer some of the richest insights into building competitive advantage in all of management. One effective tactic involves the use of countercyclically increasing advertising as a recession takes hold to take advantage of lower ad costs and reduced "noise" levels in the market. This counter-cyclical advertising helps build both brand strength and market share.

More subtly, the Master Cyclist marketer is also adept at tactically changing both the marketing messages and product mix to fit the customer's changing "moods" across the business cycle seasons.

▩ Building the Brand Through Countercyclical Advertising

- ▩ Kmart's "Mac the Knife" CEO slashes advertising during a recession and helps drive the company straight into Chapter 11 bankruptcy—with a little push from Wal-Mart.
- ▩ In the 1990-1991 recession, a then-young upstart Dell jump-starts its business with a brilliant countercyclical ad campaign.

"[W]e intend to have a record year. How? In a downturn, everyone cuts advertising. So if you just maintain advertising, you stand out. And we are going to increase our advertising."

—Jack Kahl, president and CEO, Manco Inc.

"Advertise! And better yet, advertise a lot. Why? Because, there is ample evidence to support the fact that maintaining or increasing your advertising and marketing investment in slow [recessionary] times is actually more effective than in good or growth periods. A key reason is that when the marketing and advertising "noise" goes down, the voice of those still talking sounds that much louder.

—John Kypriotakis, founder, Lysis International

Although many marketing professors and management consultants have documented the numerous benefits of countercyclical advertising in building the brand and expanding market share during a recession, surprisingly few companies and marketing practitioners actually embrace such a strategy. A major reason is that unlike the company budgets for employees, capital expenditures, and research and development, the advertising budget is fairly liquid. This liquidity makes it an easy target for the Reactive Cyclist bean counters and cost cutters when bad times hit. However, one of the most enduring lessons of the marketing literature is that *it is typically far more expensive to buy back market share lost to a rival who aggressively advertises in a downturn than it is to hold on to that market share by maintaining the marketing budget!*

The example of Kmart—whose "Mac the Knife" CEO cut advertising all the way to the Chapter 11 bankruptcy bone— illustrates the disastrous consequences that can befall a company when it procyclically slashes advertising during a recession.

Kmart Cuts Off Its Advertising Nose to Spite Its Face

"There is no doubt we made a mistake by cutting too much advertising too fast."

—**Chuck Conway, CEO, Kmart**

Chuck Conway is one of a classic breed of "ride-to-the-rescue" CEOs. In May 2000, the Kmart board of directors brought him in to perform a turnaround miracle—and within 20 months he managed to bankrupt the company, wipe out $3 billion in shareholder equity, and put 22,000 people on the unemployment lines.

At first, it seemed as if Conway was succeeding. A little less than a year after taking the company's reins, Conway boasted that "same-store sales" were rising and that the company was "building momentum." (The "yardstick" of same store sales is commonly regarded as the best measure of retail performance. It compares the sales dollars generated in the current year to the previous year.) However, Conway's boast proved empty. In fact, archrival Wal-Mart's same-store sales rose even faster, and much of the alleged momentum was merely an illusory byproduct of a white-hot economy.

With the onset of the March 2001 recession, the beleaguered Conway ordered a 30,000-item price reduction to better compete against Wal-Mart's everyday low-price strategy. This price cutting will be tactically consistent with our discussion of pricing over the course of the business cycle in the next chapter. However, in a misplaced "devil's bargain," Conway decided to "pay" for the price cuts by blatantly violating another Master Cyclist principle: He slashed Kmart's advertising budget as the recession took hold.

These steep advertising cuts came at the worst possible time for a deep-discount retailer such as Kmart. The cuts began in the summer, at a time when families were starting to do their back-to-school shopping. The cuts then accelerated into November as the crucial holiday shopping season began.

The steep advertising cuts were also administered in the worst possible way. Much of the brunt of the cuts was borne by Kmart's "Sunday circulars"—a key source of a lion's share of Kmart's sales.

Of course, while Kmart experienced a double-digit drop in weekend customer visits and sales well below target, Wal-Mart's marketing team threw ample fuel on Kmart's self-immolating fire. Wal-Mart did so by increasing its own advertising.

The result: Kmart posted a loss in sales revenue in both October and November; in contrast, Wal-Mart saw revenues increase. By January 2002, Kmart was forced to file for Chapter 11 bankruptcy.

This sordid little Reactive Cyclist story does not end just yet. In March 2002, on the one-year anniversary of the onset of the recession, Kmart's board fired Conway. However, in the Alice in Wonderland world of executive compensation, Conway's "Mac the Knife" walked off with almost $10 million.

Dell's Countercyclical Ad Coup

> *"The continued investment in marketing activities during tough economic times has really paid off for Dell."*
>
> **—Marketing Management**

As a sharp counterpoint to the foibles of Kmart, consider the brilliant countercyclical advertising coup originally responsible for jump-starting the then-young upstart Dell Computer in 1991.

During the 1990-1991 recession, advertising in the entire computer hardware industry fell by an average of almost 20 percent. The procyclical slashers fueling this downward trend included many of the biggest names in the industry at the time—from Apple and IBM to Digital.

At this propitious time, the then-upstart Dell jumped into this advertising breach with its checkbook blazing. At the very peak of the recession, it significantly increased its marketing dollars even while its competitors were quick to cut back. Without the clutter of its competitors, Dell successfully delivered its message to its customers.

This combination of countercyclical advertising and the kind of build-to-order system discussed in the preceding chapter proved to be an unbeatable combination. Within a decade, Dell vaulted to near the top of the computer heap and, as the preceding excerpt from *Marketing Management* indicates, it did so in no small part because of its bold marketing during "tough economic times."

■■■ Cycling the Product Mix and Advertising Messages

- YUM!'s Pizza Hut chain hawks its large-dish delights as a low-cost-per-slice "family meal."
- El Pollo Loco's value proposition of cheaper dark-meat specials for dark recessionary times allows this not so "Crazy Chicken" to boost revenues and profit margins.
- Centex increases the proportion of lower-cost homes in its product mix whenever a recession looms to take advantage of this more cycle-resistant market niche.

"We shift our product line with cyclical movements—particularly leveraging different cycles in different countries and moving between the public and private sectors."

—Ray Holdsworth, CEO, AECOM Technology Corp.

Not just the level of advertising expenditures should change in response to changes in customer moods through the business cycle seasons. The most sophisticated Master Cyclist marketer also understands the enormous tactical advantages of changing both the *product mix* and *marketing messages* through the business cycle seasons. The simple truth behind such tactical cycling of the mix and messages is that many consumers respond more to product value than style during recessionary times.

YUM!'s Pizza Hut Makes It a "Family Affair"

"Pizza Hut ... is secretly testing a new and permanent budget pricing strategy. It is believed to be a direct response both to the recession and to the entry of McDonald's into an already crowded market. ... Rivals are studying the Pizza Hut initiative carefully."

—Marketing Magazine

YUM! stands tall as a fast-food king, with more than 33,000 outlets in roughly 100 countries. Its marquee brands include Kentucky Fried Chicken, Taco Bell, and Long John Silver. However, YUM!'s Pizza Hut chain offers the best example of a company tactically remessaging a product during hard economic times.

To compete with low-priced local foods and other cheaper alternatives during the 2001 recession, the ever-value-conscious Hut emphasized pizza as a full meal that the family could share. It particularly highlighted pizza's low cost per person.

Taking a page out of the countercyclical advertising book, Pizza Hut also used the recessionary interlude to strengthen its brand name by ratcheting up its advertising as competitors cut theirs. In fact, Pizza Hut had used this very same Master Cyclist tactic in the

1990-1991 recession. As the bean counters at McDonald's insisted on cutting advertising, Pizza Hut increased its own. While the Hut's sales went up by more than 60 percent, Big Mac's dropped by almost 30 percent.

El Pollo Loco's Dark Meat for Dark Times

"I've never been a white-meat type, not even as a kid ... My entire nuclear and extended family lunged for drumsticks and thighs like a game of musical chicken parts. My dream bird is a flat-chested chicken with four legs."

—Author Elaine Corn, *Chicken: 150 Recipes for All Seasons*

The Master Cyclist marketer does not just change the marketing message over the course of the business cycle seasons. In some cases, the Master Cyclist marketer also changes the *product mix.* That is a lesson to be learned from the tactical gambit of another fast-food franchiser—the fast-food, flame-grilled chicken chain El Pollo Loco.

This particularly interesting example helps reinforce the point that even when a company lacks adequate forecasting capabilities and fails to anticipate a recession, the executive team can *still* use its common Master Cyclist sense to first minimize the damage—and then even prosper.

That is exactly what El Pollo Loco pulled off as the 2001 recession began to take hold. During that time, the company's executive team quickly became aware of falling demand. The team also clearly understood that the only growth the company was experiencing was coming from price *increases.* As discussed in the next chapter, this scenario represents a dangerous strategy during a recession.

Viewing this dangerous landscape, the company's anything-but-"Loco" executive team quickly tacked away from its price-hike strategy with the introduction of its first discounted-price deal in years. The promotion was a "Leg and Thighs" deal, with 10 pieces for $6.99—a very aggressive price point.

The genius of this approach from a Master Cyclist perspective is that white-meat chicken costs about 60 percent more than dark meat. By shifting its product mix toward the dark-meat end, El Pollo Loco's marketing team could pass savings along to its customers, highlight a purely price-driven promotion, and get credit with its customers for offering an abundance of food at a great value—all the while boosting profit margins!

Centex Goes Low During Recessions

"The housing industry ... is a good example of marketing management action in a recession period: Faced with growing uncertainty and slower-growing disposable income, on one hand, and the rising cost of private homes, on the other, many potential buyers left the housing market. To cope with this situation of radically declining demand, many builders adjusted their marketing mix by offering smaller, cheaper houses."

—Professor Avraham Shama[1]

Whereas El Pollo Loco lacks a sophisticated business cycle forecasting capability, the same cannot be said for Centex—the number-one homebuilder in the United States. Historically, home building, as an industry, has suffered from recessionary downturns—downturns often marked by great variations in housing market conditions across different regions.

To cope with this extreme cyclicity and regional market volatility, Centex has deployed a "decentralized" forecasting strategy in which the company is broken up into 55 divisions in 5 regions. Each division has several staff members who track local trends, and the company also tracks numerous economic indicators, with three of the most important being the jobs data, housing starts, and building permits. One virtue of this decentralized structure is that all the available forecasting information is sent up to the divisional level for analysis, after which it is sent further up the chain for national analysis.

At the first sign of any cooling in the national or a regional market, Centex typically has *increased the proportion of lower-cost homes they build.* This tactical shift in the product mix to the low end of the pricing spectrum is a function of one of the most important lessons Centex's executive team has learned after repeated experience with business cycle variations: The low-end portion of the housing market is more insulated from cyclical variations and more resilient during recessions.

■■ ■ Retargeting the Customer and Market

■ Singapore Airlines retargets its market toward first-class and full-fare customers flying transcontinental routes to smooth out the effects of business cycle volatility while boosting profit margins.

■ The Nature Conservancy's transformational retargeting of its donor base in the wake of the 2000 stock market collapse significantly boosts its donations—and shows us that Master Cycling is for nonprofit organizations, too.

A final variation on the theme of Master Cyclist marketing involves the careful retargeting of one's customers and markets as changing economic conditions warrant. The Singapore Airlines example particularly showcases this idea because it again illustrates the dangers that can arise whenever the "bean counters" launch a recessionary, cost-cutting coup. The Nature Conservancy example likewise puts an exclamation point on an equally key point, namely that Master Cyclist management is just as effective for nonprofit organizations as it is for profit-seeking companies.

Singapore Airlines Thinks Twice About Cost Cutting

"Before you pick up the hatchet, assess your customers. Identify the long-term profitability of each market segment. Should a recession hit, your best customers typically provide an even greater share of your profits, while your worst customers typical become value destroyers."

—Mercer Management Consulting

Singapore Airlines is a "limited" company with the majority shareholder being the Singapore government. This upscale carrier has roughly 100 planes and a network of routes that includes 60 cities in more than 30 countries.

The carrier's careful retargeting of its market came about quite circuitously—the unintended result of an extremely revealing customer audit. This audit unexpectedly identified the company's most profitable customers—in *both* good times and bad—as being full-fare business and first-class travelers on transcontinental routes. Based on this customer analysis, the executive team quickly came to understand that if it slashed the wrong 10 percent of its budget—for example, by cutting quality in the full-fare and first-class end—the team could destroy 100 percent of the firm's value proposition and market advantage.

The retargeting strategy that emerged from this realization was both straightforward and counterintuitive. The *straightforward* part was that the company should indeed cut costs as the bean counters were demanding, particularly during the tough economic times of the 1997-1998 Asian financial crisis. However, it should do so only in the least profitable customer segments. The *counterintuitive* part was that—to the horror of the bean counters—the company should actually spend much *more* on its more profitable full-fare and first-class transcontinental routes.

To implement this strategy—and keep peace with the bean counters—the executive team adopted a "Cut 2-Invest 1" program. The Cut 2 part of the equation involved cutting many short-haul routes to reduce costs. The Invest 1 part of the equation involved spending at least $1 for every $2 it had cut on various emoluments for its preferred customers—from more comfortable seats, sophisticated entertainment systems, and in-flight gaming to better meals and more training for flight attendants.

That this airline does indeed reflect the epitome of luxury travel targeted at the high end of the market is evident in this excerpt from one of New Zealand's leading newspapers, *The Dominion*:

> *Singapore Airlines is spending $500 million to upgrade the interiors and services of its aircraft fleet despite an expectation that it will see profits down significantly ... because of the Asian financial crisis. ... The interior redesign will see first class seating cut from 16 seats to 12 seats on its long-distance megatop 747s. The seating would be like a cross between the inside of a Rolls-Royce and a sleeper on the Orient Express train, done out in wood panels and leather, with seats that stretch out to two-metre-long beds. Business class will be cut from 65 seats to 58 in total and will also be remodeled. There will be minor remodeling in economy class.*

As an outgrowth of its retargeting strategy, Singapore Airlines was named by *Fortune* magazine as the "most admired airline" and regularly dominates the Business Traveler Asia-Pacific Travel Awards. More broadly, because of this strategic retargeting—and the stability of revenues it brings—Singapore Airlines has remained consistently profitable, even as many of other regional air carriers have been brought to their knees—first by the 1997-1998 Asian financial crisis and later by the traumatic events of 9/11.

The Nature Conservancy's Transformational Retargeting

"A major gifts staffer had been cultivating a prospective donor from a leading telecommunications company since mid-2000. By following the company, the fund-raiser knew that the stock was currently trading around its 52-week high. Utilizing the alert system in the new fund-raising software that informed the fund-raiser of a looming options expiration date, the fund-raiser was able to time the 'ask' of the donor to this expiration. The result: the donor gave several thousand shares of the stock to the Nature Conservancy and was also able to avoid some capital gains taxes."

—Cecile Richardson, The Nature Conservancy

The Nature Conservancy is a inspirational and transformational story about how the largest conservation group in the world successfully retooled and retargeted its fund-raising operation in the face of a dramatic reduction in charitable giving following the collapse of the stock market in 2000 and the ensuing 2001 recession.

For almost 50 years prior to this recession, the Nature Conservancy had conducted a very low-key fund-raising campaign. During this earlier era, the Conservancy relied primarily on a fairly laid-back direct-mail campaign and loyal membership contributions to fund its operations—with the steady stream of gifts resulting largely from an emotional connection to the "Last Great Places" the Nature Conservancy was trying to save.

In the wake of the 2000 stock market collapse, however, charitable gifts dropped precipitously. As a result of this rather urgent wake-up call, the Conservancy's executive team undertook a major strategic shift—one that had all the hallmarks of a sound Master Cyclist approach.

For starters, while many other nonprofits were laying off workers, the Conservancy actually *increased* its Major Gifts staff. Moreover, it did so in classic Master Cyclist fashion—by systematically "cherry picking" seasoned fund-raisers at bargain rates who had been laid off or recruited from foundations and other non-profits based in and around Silicon Valley.

The Conservancy also began what would be a massive and very systematic retargeting of its "customers" (that is, its *donor base*). To facilitate this effort, the Conservancy added a new Principal Gifts team to specifically retarget "high-net-worth" donors. Although high-net-worth donors represent only 2 percent of donors, they typically account for 90 percent of all private fund-raising dollars!

Perhaps most inventively, the Conservancy also instituted several programs to cultivate a Master Cyclist perspective in its fund-raising team. One program allowed its Principal Gifts staff to order an individual allowance of subscriptions each year to financial resources such as the *Wall Street Journal, Forbes*, and *Barron's*. This subscription effort was not just to improve their business cycle and financial market literacy. It was also to help them think like their donors.

A second Strategic Gifts Training program featured a seminar on how the movements of various important leading economic indicators might affect the timing and type of charitable giving for which the fund-raisers would be asking. That these kinds of programs turned out to be quite valuable is evident in the preceding excerpt from Cecile Richardson that led off this example.

As for the happy ending to this Master Cyclist story, the Annual Chronicle for Philanthropy's Top 400 ranks the fund-raising totals of the major charitable organizations. Between 1999 and 2002, *before* the Nature Conservancy had fully retargeted its donor base, it ranked between number 10 and number 14. However, *after* the new business cycle-sensitive and stock market cycle-sensitive systems were inaugurated, the Conservancy significantly raised its contributions in 2003 and jumped to number 8 on the list—sandwiched neatly between the powerhouse YMCA and the philanthropic Trojans of the University of Southern California.

Key Points

- **Master Cyclist Marketing**
  - The Master Cyclist marketing team aggressively embraces *counter*cyclical advertising. It also changes both the product mix and marketing messages through the business cycle seasons and retargets the customer and the market with changing economic conditions.
- **Building the Brand Through Countercyclical Advertising**
  - Increasing advertising during a recession can be a highly effective way of building the brand and increasing market share because ad rates are cheaper and there is less "noise" in the marketplace.
  - Despite compelling evidence that countercyclical advertising is a highly effective strategy, many companies do not embrace it because the "bean counters" find the advertising budget to be one of the easiest cost-cutting targets in a recession.
- **Cycling the Product Mix and Advertising Messages**
  - Because consumers respond more to product value than to style in recessionary times, it is important to tailor both the advertising messages and product mix to best fit the "moods" of the different business cycle seasons.
- **Retargeting the Customer and Market**
  - Movements in the business cycle, and the related stock market and interest rate cycles, can often trigger the need to retarget one's customers or one's market.

7

Pricing the Cycle and Managing Credit and Accounts Receivable

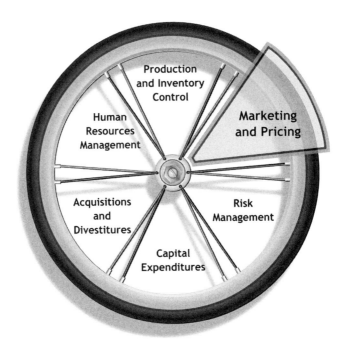

"Knowing the elasticity of demand for your products ... is a key to determining pricing strategy."

—James Stotter, founder, Busimetrics

"... when money is abundant, consumers will accept almost any price increase for popular products; but when money is short, demand for many products becomes price elastic. *Cost-plus pricing, which ignores [how price elasticities change over the business cycle], has proven disastrous...."*

—Professor Edward Cundiff, *Journal of Marketing*

To understand how the Master Cyclist executive "prices the cycle," it is useful to first come to understand more about one of the most difficult but important concepts in all of economics: *price elasticity.*

Put simply, price elasticity measures how sensitive buyers are to changes in price. If price elasticity is low or *inelastic*, a big price hike will result in only a small drop in demand. Such is the case for price-inelastic necessities such as drugs for an addict, gasoline for a suburban commuter, or doctors' services for the seriously ill.

In contrast, a highly *elastic* demand means just the opposite—a small price increase can mean a big drop in purchases. Restaurant meals, airline travel, and fresh vegetables are all highly price elastic either because consumers can readily find substitutes or just do without them if prices rise too high.

Now here's the first important point to grasp: Most business executives who learned about price elasticities in their college economics courses come away with the impression that for any given product, these elasticities are *fixed*. In fact, such *elasticities can vary significantly across the business cycle.* In particular, during recessions, the price elasticities of many products will fall, whereas during strong expansions, elasticities often rise.

Why this is so should be both logical and intuitive. As the words of Professor Edward Cundiff in the preceding excerpt indicate, when times are good in a rapidly expanding economy, consumers "are willing to accept almost any price increase for popular products"; this behavior means that demand becomes more price inelastic. However, during recessions, "when money is short" and the job situation turns uncertain, consumers become much more value oriented and less willing to spend, indicating a higher, more elastic demand.

Now here is the second really important point—as well as one of the most important principles in economics: *Raising prices in the face of "price-elastic" product demand will **decrease**—not increase—profits!* This is because when demand is elastic, an increase in revenues from a price hike is more than offset by a fall in the number of goods actually sold.

Unfortunately, this critical lesson often goes unheeded by desperate Reactive Cyclist executives in a recession who try to compensate for falling revenues by raising prices in the face of increasingly elastic demand.

In contrast, the Master Cyclist marketing team recognizes this key economic principle as well as the often subtle shifts in price elasticities over the business cycle. That's why it typically raises prices in good expansionary times to boost revenues and cuts prices in bad recessionary times to protect or build market share.

■■■ The Dollars and Sense of Procyclical Pricing

- A desperate Goodyear repeatedly ratchets up tire prices into the teeth of a recession and loses a ton of money and market share.

- In a great diaper war skirmish, a too-clever-by-half Kimberly-Clark launches a "stealth" price hike attack and gets its head handed to it on a platter by a ferociously counterattacking Procter & Gamble.

- As a recession looms, Arden Realty begins reeling in its accounts receivable and leasing not to the highest-bidding tenants but rather to those with the best credit histories who will be best able to withstand an economic downturn.

Goodyear's Price Gougers Snatch Defeat from the Jaws of Victory

"We will be aggressive in increasing prices where market conditions allow."

—Goodyear 2000 Annual Report

"During 2001, we increased tire prices in markets around the world. ... Our sales declined."

—Goodyear 2001 Annual Report

Goodyear is the largest tire maker in the United States and ranks number three in the world behind Michelin and Bridgestone. The behavior of its executive team as the economy entered the 2001 recession provides a classic case of desperate Reactive Cyclist executives foolishly attempting to both raise prices in a recession and repeal an important law in economics.

Goodyear's desperation started with a heavy debt load assumed in the 1990s and a collateral liquidity problem. It escalated in

2000 with a weakening of the euro, which cut deeply into the company's profits in its European markets.[1] Desperation then hit warp speed in late 2000 as oil prices soared. This resulted in severe cost pressures on Goodyear because fully 65 percent of the raw materials used to make a tire are derived from crude oil.

As an offset to this misfortune, however, Goodyear received a huge windfall in August 2000 as rival Bridgestone announced the recall of more than 6 million tires because of blowouts that had caused more than 100 deaths. In the wake of the Bridgestone recall, Goodyear tire shipments in the North American replacement market grew at a pace almost *five* times that of the overall market, and Goodyear's executive team thought that this would be a great opportunity to raise prices.

Perhaps the team was right—at least initially. However, Goodyear executives soon ignored their own sound advice. This advice is evident in the first excerpt leading off this example in which the team promises to "be aggressive in increasing prices" *but* only "when market conditions warrant." Unfortunately, with the onset of the recession in 2001, market conditions changed dramatically, particularly for a company like Goodyear in a highly cyclical industry.

Not only did tire demand in Goodyear's replacement market fall significantly. The demand for new vehicles—and the tires they run on—softened, too. Seemingly oblivious to these sharply deteriorating market conditions, Goodyear's executive team nonetheless insisted on piling up the price hikes—three times in all in 2001!

The predictable Reactive Cyclist result: Goodyear's desperately greedy price gouging did not increase revenues, and the company lost more than $200 million. Nor did the company even gain market share from Bridgestone—Michelin got that with more competitive prices. Instead, Goodyear's stockholders saw the value of their shares plummet from a high of $31 per share in 2000 to less than $7 by 2002. As the final exclamation point to this sordid lesson in procyclical pricing, the company halved its dividend in October 2001 and eliminated it in 2002.

A "Diaper Skirmish" Between Procter & Gamble and Kimberly-Clark

"We have a philosophy and a strategy. When times are tough, you build share."

—A. J. Lafley, CEO, Procter & Gamble

While Goodyear's executive team was getting it wrong, Procter & Gamble's was getting it ever so right in a ferocious "diaper skirmish" with archrival Kimberly-Clark. This example further highlights the Reactive Cyclist dangers of trying to raise prices to boost revenues in recession even as it reinforces the Master Cyclist wisdom of cutting prices in recessionary times to build share. Here's how this very short and bittersweet story unfolded.[2]

With profits sagging from recessionary conditions, Kimberly-Clark launched a sneak attack on the working mothers of America. It indirectly raised diaper prices for its Huggies brand by reducing the number in a package.

Procter & Gamble immediately responded to this stealth price hike with a "shock-and-awe" advertising and marketing blitz aimed at exposing the smaller Huggies packs and urging customers to compare them with P&G's cheaper Pampers. As a key part of this strategy, P&G cut its own prices to further accentuate Kimberly-Clark's price hike. It also included special displays in retail outlets and the awarding of some "in-your-face" discount coupons for Pampers to anyone who bought a box of Huggies.

Eventually, Kimberly-Clark's CEO, Thomas J. Falk, had to cry "Uncle." He rescinded the price hike—but not before P&G had grabbed valuable share.

Arden Realty Downshifts to Lower Business Cycle Risk

"Arden Realty did not lease to the highest bidder or the largest tenant but to the tenants with proven performance, credit quality, and long-term leasing ability. In doing so, Arden lowered its risk ...."

—Christopher Hartung, analyst, Wells Fargo Securities

The example of Arden Realty further raises the level of sophistication of well-timed pricing strategies implemented in anticipation of recessions, and anyone who has ever driven in Southern California has certainly had time to gaze from the gridlock at one of Arden Realty's real estate investment trust properties. They are all quality, well-located buildings housing the region's top businesses—about 120 commercial properties and almost 19 million square feet of rentable office space in all.

At the beginning of 2000, as the supply of office space began to be squeezed by the demands of a hot economy, a Reactive Cyclist executive team would likely have taken the occasion to push through very hefty tenant rent increases every time a lease was renewed.

Not so Arden Realty's CEO, Richard Ziman, and his Master Cyclist executive team. They took just the opposite approach. They believed that because the Federal Reserve was continuing to relentlessly hike interest rates, a recession might well be on the way and turn the situation quickly around in a real estate sector highly sensitive to interest rates.

Accordingly, as noted in the preceding excerpt, Arden began to renew its leases *not* with the highest-bidding tenants in mind. Rather, Arden much preferred those tenants who, over the course of any economic downturn, would be best able to maintain a five-year lease. In effect, this well-timed strategy combined a rent stabilization approach with a credit-screening mechanism designed to reduce recessionary risk and maintain high occupancy rates.

In conjunction with this pricing policy, the company also began to pursue collection of its accounts receivable much more aggressively. By the end of 2001, Ziman proudly pronounced, "We have significantly decreased our receivables and currently have less than $250,000 in net receivables more than 60 days outstanding."

This part of the Arden story serves as a useful segue to a second aspect of the pricing-the-cycle equation: the collateral managing of credit and accounts receivable.

▪▪▪ Playing the Accordion of Accounts Receivable and Credit

- ▪ A cavalier Lucent embraces a "take whatever you want and pay me later" credit policy and gets stiffed by a bevy of dot.com start-ups.
- ▪ In a bonfire of Reactive Cyclist vanities, Finova self-immolates on a pyre of uncollected accounts.

In a common variation on the classical business cycle trap, it is not just overproduction, excess inventory, and idle workers that are problematic when a recession hits. Very often, in the heady and often overheated days of a late-term expansion, corporations become extremely lax about extending credit and reeling in their accounts receivable. The paradox here is that the piling up of accounts receivable is one of the first symptoms of a coming recession and can be a valuable "in-house" leading indicator—if only the management team pays attention.

More broadly, to the Master Cyclist, the timely management of credit and receivables most resembles metaphorically that of an "accordion." That is, the Master Cyclist loosens credit and allows receivables to build in anticipation of an expansion. However, credit is quickly tightened, and the collection of receivables is accelerated in anticipation of a recession.

The hapless—and extremely reckless!—Reactive Cyclists at Lucent Technologies and Finova illustrate the dire consequences of violating these rules.

Lucent's Ultra-Easy Credit Policies Lose Billions

> *"The industry in which we operate has never been more dynamic. At a growth rate of more than 14 percent a year, the market will approach $815 billion by 2003. That growth is being propelled by customer demand for next-generation networks: converged networks that deliver new services in any form—voice, data, or video. This is creating a wealth of opportunity for Lucent."*
>
> **—Richard McGinn, chairman and CEO,**
> **Lucent Technologies**

This excerpt from Lucent's 1999 Annual Report perfectly captures the utterly false sense of confidence the company maintained as the tech bubble began to burst. Within two years, this is a company that would be writing-down—and attempting to bury deep in its financial statements—more than $3 *billion* of uncollected receivables!

The grim irony of this situation should not be lost on anyone. Before its descent into penny-stock oblivion, the telecom network gear provider Lucent had one of the finest pedigrees in corporate America. It was spun off from AT&T back in 1996, and the company took with it one of the most powerful engines of innovation the world has ever seen. This was the vaunted Bell Labs—responsible for innovations ranging from the transistor and lasers to cell phone technology, communications satellites, and, yes, that miracle called the touchtone phone. No company should have had a brighter future in a world of rapid technological change.

As to how Lucent's stock price wound up plummeting from more than $60 at its peak in 2000 to *literally* pennies, there were a number of important factors. For starters, like Cisco and many other tech companies, Lucent fell prey to the classic bullwhip effect (discussed in Chapter 5, "'Macromanaging' Your Production, Inventory, and Supply Chain") and built up excess inventories on the basis of inflated demand forecasts. Like its archrival Nortel (discussed in Chapter 3, "The Acquisitive Master Cyclist Buys Low and Sells High"), the company also went on a high-priced acquisition binge and then compounded the problem by financing many of its acquisitions with high-priced debt.

Still, one of the most subtle but important contributing factors to Lucent's fall from tech-darling grace was its abysmal handling of its credit and accounts receivable. Right into the very teeth of the recession, Lucent continued to offer huge financing packages to high-risk, start-up companies to win market share and increase sales revenues. In effect, the company was saying "here, take whatever gear you want now and just pay us later"—oblivious to the mounting risk of default.

Of course, when many of these dot-com enterprises went belly-up, Lucent was unable to collect these receivables. This bad debt—along with its debt-driven acquisition hangover—left Lucent in an extremely cash-strapped position. This, in turn, hindered the ability of the company to continue their research and development responsible for its original competitive advantage—or even pay its employees.

As a final comment on this Reactive Cyclist disaster, anyone reading Lucent's annual reports will find it exceedingly difficult to pinpoint this receivables problem. One year the company states it has more than $8.8 billion of receivables on its balance sheet. The next year that figure has miraculously shrunk to $4.6 billion.

Did the company collect all of these *billions*? Absolutely not. Did the company clearly explain where the money went? Hardly.

In fact, in one of the most blatant examples of a desperate management team trying to bury its mistakes deep into its balance sheet, Lucent shifted more than $3 billion of its uncollected receivables out of what is a very prominent balance sheet item—accounts receivable—and into several other lower-profile assets such as "reserves against receivables" and "bad debt charges." The company also appears to have used some highly creative accounting—for example, creating an obscure "qualified special-purpose entity"—to likewise move another big chunk of its receivables out of plain sight.

Fortunately, investors did not need Sherlock Holmes or a forensic accountant to tell them this company was in desperate straits. They bailed out faster than you can say "penny stock"—the accounting charade notwithstanding.

Finova's Bonfire of the Reactive Cyclist Vanities

> "Hedging of business cycle risk was thought to have been accomplished by creating numerous lending divisions … that focused on different industries; i.e., health care, time share, hospitality, franchise restaurants, etc. Unfortunately, in each case we were lending to the unbankable borrowers within each industry group, which all would have financial difficulties during a general down business cycle. While our senior management team was well read, they did not publicly give attention to macroeconomic and financial news."

—Glenn Gray, COO, Finova

The name *Finova* was originally coined from the amalgam of *financial* and *innovators*. A better name might have been *Finicide* crafted from the words *financial* and *suicide*. This is because Finova self-immolated in the most spectacular of fashions. It did so by building a business model doomed to incinerate in the bonfires of recession and sharply rising interest rates.

Finova started out first as a subsidiary of the Greyhound bus company in 1954, was later acquired by the Dial Corporation, and eventually was spun off from Dial in 1992. It wasn't until 1995, however, that Finova really kicked into high-gear growth. This is when Finova's growth-obsessed CEO, Sam Eichenfield, began an acquisition binge that quickly grew the company's loan portfolio from a few billion dollars to more than $13 billion. In the process, this growth elevated the company to the prestigious Forbes Platinum 400 list by 2000—a list that, at least in theory, was supposed to identify "the best companies in America."

As to what exactly Finova was doing to earn its Forbes stripes, well, that is a very sobering lesson in the relationship of risk to reward. As an ironclad rule of finance, the more risk you are willing to take on, the higher your possible reward—but also the greater the chance of punishing losses. That was ultimately Finova's undoing; because to maintain Eichenfield's hyper rate of profitability growth, the company's minions had to take on huge risks.

In this regard, Finova's self-defined market niche as a commercial lender was to offer lavish credit to extremely high-risk ventures. As the *New York Times* succinctly described Finova's customer base, it consisted of those companies that were "too small, too new, or too indebted to go to banks."

Of course, it was precisely because Finova's clients were so desperate to obtain credit that Finova could charge them such high interest rates. There is nothing wrong with that *per se*— unless you take a biblical view of the sins of usury. What was, however, so very wrong with Finova was how the company blatantly ignored the dynamics of the interest rate cycle as it generated its loanable funds.

Unlike banks, which derive a majority of their loanable funds from customer deposits, Finova first had to borrow all the money that it would, in turn, lend out. At least on the surface, it did so in much the same way that that you will see Countrywide Financial do in the next chapter—borrowing at lower interest rates, lending high, and then earning profits on the "spread."

A big difference with Finova's strategy, however, is that it lacked any of the interest rate hedging mechanisms that Countrywide embraced. Indeed, running naked to the winds of risk, Finova chose to obtain the bulk of its funds from short-term commercial paper that had expirations of one year or less. In this way, Finova could maximize the spread between the short-term funds it borrowed and the long-term funds it lent. But *this was true only as long as the spread between short- and long-term rates remained comfortably wide.*

This combination of targeting high-risk borrowers, running unhedged, offering lavish credit, and borrowing short term to fund its long-term growth would prove to be absolutely incendiary when the Federal Reserve began raising short-term rates and the economy began to slow. In effect, the spark for the bonfires that followed was Finova's complete lack of understanding of how a downturn in the business cycle and an upward swing in the interest rate cycle could bankrupt the company *in a matter of months.*

The first flames to be lit on Finova came from the business cycle. As the economy softened, one of Finova's largest single borrowers defaulted on a huge loan. This default forced Finova to take an astonishing $70 million charge on its earnings.

At this very same time, like a rat leaving a soon-to-be-sinking ship, Finova's CEO took an early retirement. Eichenfield's retirement was not just a strong signal to the lending community that something might be desperately wrong with the Finova house of cards. Eichenfield also sucked another $10 million out in severance pay on his way out the door.

Together, these charges and Eichenfield's suspiciously timed exit first caused the company to miss its first quarter 2000 earnings goals and then ignited a plunge in the company's stock price. In this same time frame, Finova's own lenders suddenly became more wary of lending Finova any more money—at least someone knew how to tighten credit in a recession!

Perhaps even worse, Finova's own credit rating was significantly downgraded. That meant it would have to pay much more for its increasingly scarce loanable funds.

Together, this sudden turn of events could not have come at a worst time in the interest rate cycle. As the Fed inexorably turned up the short-term interest rate screws, as the economy steadily softened, and as its own interest rate costs rose, Finova saw its profit spread between short- and long-run rates evaporate.

As its short-term paper became due, Finova was unable to secure additional debt financing, and this final squeeze ultimately spelled the end of Finova as a working concern—ironically a little more than a year after the company's "coronation" by Forbes on the Platinum 400 list.

One final Master Cyclist observation might be worthwhile here: A Master Cyclist view of what happened to Finova is that its executive team just did not understand how to manage a financial concern through movements in the business cycle, interest rate cycle, and stock market cycle. This view is bolstered not just by the company's actions, but also by the excerpt leading off this example from Finova's COO.

In that candid appraisal, Glenn Gray reveals how *the executive team actually believed it was well hedged with respect to business cycle risk because its loan portfolio was spread across many different industries.* However, what the team did not understand is that by focusing on the highest-risk lenders in each of these industries, "all would have financial difficulties during a general downturn." In this scenario, having a true Master Cyclist on Finova's team might have saved it from its own self-immolating end.

Key Points

- **Pricing the Cycle and Managing Receivables**
  - Price elasticity measures how sensitive buyers are to changes in price. If demand is *inelastic*, a big price hike will result in only a small drop in demand, whereas a highly *elastic* demand means just the opposite—a small price increase means a big drop in purchases.
  - One of the most important principles in economics is that raising prices in the face of price-elastic demand will *decrease*—not increase—profits!
  - Reactive Cyclist executives often ignore this principle and try to compensate for falling revenues during a recession by raising prices when elasticities are rising.

- **The Dollars and Sense of Procyclical Pricing**
  - During recessions, "when money is short" and the job situation turns uncertain, consumers become much more value oriented and demand becomes more highly "elastic" or price sensitive. This is the best time to cut prices to protect or build market share.
  - The Master Cyclist executive cuts prices in bad recessionary times to protect or build market share and raises prices in good expansionary times to boost revenues.

- **Managing Credit and Accounts Receivable**
  - The Master Cyclist tightens credit and more aggressively reels in accounts receivable in anticipation of a recession.

▄▄▀ Author's Note on the "Master Cyclist Risk Management Wheel"

Before moving on to the next three chapters on risk management, you might find it useful to briefly review the figure on the opposite page. It illustrates the three major components of the Master Cyclist "risk management wheel"—an important companion to the more general Master Cyclist management wheel.

As you can see in the right portion of the figure, one important area of risk management involves the hedging of general business cycle risk. This is typically accomplished by using tools such as business unit and geographical diversification.

A second risk management area involves hedging—and often opportunistically *leveraging*—the more specific risks associated with movements in commodity and oil prices, interest rates, and exchange rates. This is usually done using various "financial derivatives" such as call options and futures.

Finally, a third major source of risk that can jolt even the healthiest of business cycle expansions into a recession includes a wide variety of so-called *exogenous shocks*. Such random external shocks to the economy range from war and terrorism and drought and disease to earthquakes and tsunamis. Grim though this observation might be, the onset of such shocks nonetheless often creates opportunities for the Master Cyclist executive team to develop new products or markets or simply to retarget old markets.

The Master Cyclist Risk Management Wheel

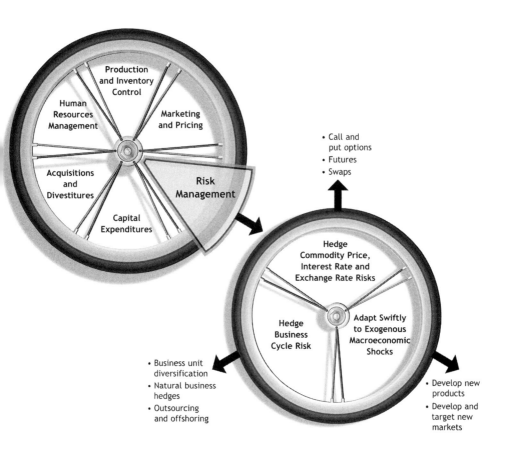

Proactive Profiting from Oil Price Spikes, Interest Rate Hikes, and Exchange Rate Risks

"Union Special [was a] small, Chicago-based manufacturer of sewing machines. Its sales were in the $100 million per year range and until the late 1980s it had no explicit foreign exchange rate risk strategy. But ... by doing nothing it actually did have a strategy; i.e., it bet the entire company on the changes in the floating exchange rate. ... The result was major losses and ... the company was taken over by Japanese buyers. [emphasis added]

—**Professor Thayer Watkins**[1]

Manufacturing companies like General Motors, Eastman Kodak, and General Mills are heavily dependent on the cost of raw materials such as steel, silver, and wheat. Multinational companies like Caterpillar and McDonald's that produce or sell their products across countries and regions must navigate an intricate web of exchange rate risks. And all companies—but particularly financial institutions—are exposed to the often substantial risks associated with interest rate volatility.

As the preceding excerpt underscores, companies like Union Special that ignore such "macroeconomic" risks nonetheless *still* have a strategy! However, as Union Special painfully found out, such a *de facto* "do-nothing" strategy can often lead straight to huge losses and a loss of autonomy.

To manage—and leverage—the specific risks associated with movements in commodity prices, exchange rates, and interest rates, the Master Cyclist executive team has a wide range of "risk-hedging" tools at its disposal. These tools necessarily include the deployment of "financial derivatives" such as futures and options and swaps—which you will see skillfully employed by companies such as Good Humor-Breyers, Southwest Airlines, and Royal Caribbean Cruises. However, the Master Cyclist team is also highly skilled in constructing natural "business hedges" that can help balance out risks—as demonstrated by the virtuoso performance of Countrywide Financial.

As a cautionary note, you will also see with Procter & Gamble why companies should never gamble heavily with derivatives, but merely use them for hedging. You will likewise see with Washington Mutual how a seemingly savvy management team with the best of hedging intentions still somehow went astray. The culprit: an overambitious acquisitions program that stretched the company far beyond its hedging limits.

■■■ Hedging Commodity Prices and Oil Price Shocks

- Good Humor-Breyers uses sophisticated industry-specific analysis to strategically hedge the costs of key ingredients such as butterfat and vanilla for its heart-stopping ice cream brands.
- Southwest Airlines' "tactical opportunists" shrewdly exploit the company's sophisticated forecasting capabilities to adjust their fuel hedges as conditions warrant—and stay three steps ahead of their competitors and the OPEC cartel.

"For the past hundred years, candy companies have faced 'the problem of selling a product in intensely competitive conditions at a fixed shelf price but having to buy their raw materials such as cocoa and sugar in a wildly fluctuating commodity market...'
The companies have responded by setting up 'highly sophisticated and well-funded hedging departments' to get the best prices for their inputs. That has meant relatively stable product prices and preparedness in the war for market share..."

—Metals Week

The New England Confectionary Company uses about 100 tons of granular sugar a *day* to make its "NECCO wafers" and other sweets. General Motors uses about 6 million tons of steel a year for its car, truck, and SUV production, and the U.S. airline industry annually burns through about 20 *billion* gallons of jet fuel.

Given these magnitudes, it is no wonder that one of the biggest challenges many companies face is hedging the costs of such raw materials. One common method to hedge such commodity price risk is through the use of "financial derivatives" such as futures and options. These risk-hedging tools enable companies to "lock in" a particular price for a raw material and thereby guarantee "stable product prices."

Of course, if the market price turns out to be lower than the hedged price, a company loses on the hedge. However, a small hedging loss is often far preferable to a much larger loss that can come about if the price of a particular raw material soars.

In the examples of both Good Humor-Breyers and Southwest Airlines, we will see two companies use highly sophisticated forecasting tools as the prelude to employing their hedging strategies and tactics. But there is an important difference between these two companies.

Whereas Good Humor-Breyers opts for a complete *strategic* hedge for its key ice cream ingredients, Southwest Airlines illustrates a more nimble *tactical* opportunism. That is, although virtually *all* airlines maintain a partial hedge against fuel price increases, Southwest has tactically increased its hedging at key intervals when its macroeconomic forecasting models suggested an approaching oil price spike. This kind of proactive and tactical opportunism is the true mark of a Master Cyclist.

Good Humor-Breyers—Serious as a Heart Attack About Butterfat

> *"Butterfat, the essence of junk food, is in short supply because manufacturers have been using more of it over the past couple of years, responding to the public's demand for richer foods and the rejection of low-calorie products, which are often low on taste."*
>
> *—**Boston Globe***

Famous for both its Good Humor bars and Popsicles, Good Humor-Breyers is the largest ice cream manufacturer and marketer in the good-old high-cholesterol U.S. of A. Although many people view the primary risk of a key ingredient such as butterfat to be heart disease, Good Humor-Breyers sees the real risk to its bottom line.

Consider that just a one cent change in the price of butter fat can move the company's annual profits by half a million dollars. That's why Good Humor-Breyers' annual shopping hunt for its all-important cheap butterfat is conducted with all the precision of a Space Shuttle launch and all the zeal of a missionary.

As for what moves the price of butterfat, certainly *part* of the movement is related to the general business cycle. However, this is a good example of how cyclical risk is also tied to the often "boom-and-bust" movements of *specific-industry cycles*, in this case, the dairy sector.

To manage this type of supply chain risk, Good Humor-Breyers first prepares a conservative annual plan based on prior-year prices for butterfat as well as a thorough "macro" analysis of the industry. This macro analysis includes such factors as the levels of cheese production, butterfat production and costs, and cow production in terms of both headcount and yield per cow.

After the team has an idea of forecast prices, it then goes about the business of trying to lock in the prices through the use of futures contracts early in the year. And note that it's not just butterfat risk that this company seeks to hedge. With more than half of the world's vanilla bean crop coming from two very remote and politically unstable islands in the Indian Ocean—Madagascar and Comoros—the company's executive team also employs a similar strategy for this very crucial "raw material" of ice cream.

Southwest Airlines' Stays Three Steps Ahead of OPEC

> *"No savings is too small these days in the global airline industry, where an unforeseen spike in crude oil prices has added billions of dollars to fuel tabs and forced carriers to turn to innovative—and sometimes desperate—measures to cut consumption, drop by drop."*
>
> **—Aviation Week & Space Technology**

Much of Southwest Airlines' success—more than 30 consecutive years of profitability at last count!—stems from a value proposition that features a low-budget, no-assigned-seats approach, a ticketless travel system that keeps its "back-office" costs low, a series of charismatic CEOs, and a unique organizational culture renown for its humor and high employee morale.

That said, Southwest Airlines also offers an example of a hard-nosed Master Cyclist that relies heavily on macroeconomic forecasting to manage all phases of its business. The company's own internal model is highly sophisticated and incorporates not only various aspects of global supply and demand, monetary aggregates, and exchange rates, but also assessments of geopolitical risk. This forecasting model has proved particularly useful in Southwest's fuel cost hedging tactics.

In this regard, fuel costs constitute about 15 percent of a revenue dollar for most airlines—second only to the cost of labor.

Although almost all airline companies strategically engage in some fuel cost hedging, most typically only hedge less than *half*—and often well less than half—of their fuel needs.

However, the Master Cyclist Southwest frequently, opportunistically, and *tactically* departs from this industry practice when its macro models tell it to do so. A particularly profitable case in point: In early 2000, Southwest's executive team opted for a close to 100 percent fuel hedge for the third and fourth quarters based on an internal forecast of a significant shortage of crude oil. As oil prices soared above $30, Southwest used a complex array of financial derivatives to save more than $110 million in fuel costs and saw its earnings increase for the year by more than 30 percent—almost three times the industry average.

This is hardly the only instance where Southwest got its fuel hedge right. In the second half of 2004, when oil prices soared past the $50 per-barrel mark, Southwest had a full 80 percent of its fuel costs hedged at a price of $24 per barrel. This contrasted sharply with three other "legacy" airlines: Continental had a 45 percent hedge at $36, Northwest had a 25 percent hedge at from $34 to $41, and Delta was *completely unhedged.*[2]

Royal Caribbean's Captains Remain Calm During War's Chaos

> *"Royal Caribbean Cruise Lines spends a lot of money at the fuel dock; but even though petroleum prices have soared to their highest levels in five years, all is calm at the company's Miami headquarters; that's because of a risk-management tool called commodity swaps; months before Iraq overran Kuwait, Royal Caribbean used this tool to hedge against price increases for much of its fuel needs this year and beyond."*
>
> **—Wall Street Journal**

Royal Caribbean Cruises (RCC) is the second largest cruise ship line in the world. Its vast fleet entertains more than two million passengers a year in destinations that range from Alaska and Europe to, you guessed it, the Caribbean.

The preceding excerpt from the *Wall Street Journal*, circa 1990, provides a brief but telling historical portrait of a Master Cyclist at the top of its hedging game. But Royal Caribbean's success at hedging its fuel costs during the first war with Iraq was hardly an anomaly.

In 1999, the company's forecasting model predicted a high probability of increasing oil prices. In response, its executive team hedged between 10 percent and 30 percent of its fuel costs over the next three years. This tactical hedge enabled RCC to keep its fuel costs under 7 percent of operating expenses—one of the best in the industry.

With kudos thus delivered on the oil price shock front, Royal Caribbean is, however, much more a story about how this company has hedged a massive *currency risk* during an equally massive expansion that vaulted the cruise line to its coveted position in the industry today—a story to which we now turn.

Hedging the Many Faces of Exchange Rate Risk

- The captains of industry at Royal Caribbean find calm economic seas in both war and peacetime by buying euro-priced cruise ships with fully hedged dollars.
- Procter & Gamble's "dumb and dumber" gamble against the (Bankers Trust) "house" offers a painful lesson in why most companies should limit their use of financial derivatives to risk hedging instead of engaging in highly leveraged gambling.

> *"Sir Freddie Laker ... pioneered low-cost trans-Atlantic travel. He primarily sold American vacations to British travelers. He started out at a time when the pound was strong and the dollar weak. Business was good, and he contracted to buy American aircraft at a price set in dollars. When the dollar strengthened, not only was his pound revenue worth less in terms of dollars, so more pounds had to be devoted to paying for the new planes, but the weaker pound resulted in less travel. Laker had fewer pounds but a bigger bill for the planes. The result was bankruptcy."*
>
> **—Professor Thayer Watkins**

One of the least understood—but often most important—risks that companies face in an increasingly global economy is that of "exchange rate risk." This kind of risk can wear many faces—two of which, as Sir Freddy Laker painfully found out, are "translation risk" and "transactions risk."[3]

To understand *translation* risk, suppose your company is based in the United States but sells many of its products in Europe. If the European currency weakens, your net profits from foreign operations will go down. This is because to "repatriate" those profits from Europe, you have exchange the weaker euro for a stronger dollar. This is the "translation effect"—the effect of converting a currency such as the euro earned abroad into dollars. Because of this *translation risk*, many multinational companies— from McDonald's and Merck to BMW and Toyota—use currency market futures as a hedge against exchange rate risk.

As for *transaction* risk, suppose your company is based in the United Kingdom like Laker Airlines was. However, to do your business, you must buy significant amounts of capital equipment from the United States—say, a fleet of planes from America's Boeing Corporation. If you contractually commit to paying for the planes in dollars upon delivery—*but* that delivery will not occur for several years and the dollar appreciates against the pound— you will get stuck with a much bigger bill than you anticipated.

You might even wind up in bankruptcy as a result—just as Freddy Laker did.

So how do you avoid such a disaster? Royal Caribbean shows us at least one way.

Royal Caribbean Charts a Euro-Dollar Hedging Course

> *"Buoyed by the success of the revolutionary cruise ship* Voyager of the Seas, *Royal Caribbean Cruises ... and [Finish shipbuilder] Kvaerner Masa-Yards have reached a preliminary agreement to build the fourth and fifth Eagle-class vessels for Royal Caribbean International. The companies have signed a letter of intent which calls for two unnamed ships at a total contract price of 1.1 billion euros, which at today's exchange rate has a value of about 1.1 billion [dollars]."*
>
> **—PR Newswire**

Royal Caribbean did not get to be the second biggest cruise ship line overnight. Rather, the company's rise to prominence began in the early 1990s when it kicked off its massive expansion.

Between 1995 and 2003, it increased its fleet size almost sixfold by buying its new ships from Europe. Each ship took about two years to build at a cost of about half a billion dollars; and to get these ships built, Royal Caribbean had to sign multiple-ship and multiple-year contracts on a regular basis and agree to pay for the ships in euros.

To hedge its huge exchange rate risk exposure, the company's executive team regularly deploys an array of financial derivatives. The important point to note here is that *by taking this kind of specific risk out of play, Royal Caribbean can focus entirely on its core competency*: filling its ships with people and feeding and entertaining them well!

I should note here, particularly for those readers who might have a jaundiced view of financial derivatives, that this type of conservative risk hedging differs significantly from the speculative use of derivatives by companies that often have no business even dipping their toe in those waters—as our next example involving Procter & Gamble demonstrates.

Procter & Gamble Gambles Against the (Banker's Trust) House

"[D]erivatives are financial weapons of mass destruction, carrying dangers that, while now latent, are potentially lethal."

—Warren Buffett

Sometimes even one of the richest men in the world—for example, the inestimable Mr. Buffett—can simply be wrong. Financial derivatives, *per se*, are not dangerous at all when properly used to hedge risk. In fact, the use of financial derivatives to manage risk dates back at least to seventeenth-century Japan, when rice futures were used to protect sellers from either war or bad weather.[4]

Where Buffett is right, however, is when financial derivatives are misused in highly speculative ventures by government entities like Orange County, California, rogue bond traders like Nick Leeson of Barings Bank, and even Nobel Laureate experts in option pricing theory running a hedge fund like Long-Term Capital Management. In each of these cases, the resultant speculative losses ran into the billions—and the Nobel Laureates almost brought the international monetary system crashing down.[5]

It would seem, then, by these big-stake standards, that Procter & Gamble's loss of $157 million in 1994 might not even be worth mentioning. At the time, however, this loss was a corporate record. More broadly, this example does raise the question as to why a company in as staid and defensive an industry as diapers and toilet tissue found itself neck deep in interest rate derivatives effectively "betting against the house."

The house in question was Bankers Trust. P&G's bet in question was that interest rates would remain stable. However, if interest rates rose, P&G would lose a bundle to Banker's Trust. This is because P&G had used the derivatives to heavily leverage its bet with Bankers Trust by an astonishing 20 to 1.

This deal raises an obvious question: How dumb do you have to be to bet against a *bank* on the future course of interest rates? But weep not for P&G. It wound up suing Bankers Trust on the grounds that it really was too dumb to do what it did—and that Bankers Trust should have warned it of the risk. For its stupidity, P&G wound up settling with Bankers Trust for a net $78 million gain.[6]

The lesson here, however, is not that the legal system always rewards stupidity. Rather, it is that unless you are in the derivatives business, your company might want to confine its use of financial derivatives to simple hedges rather than highly leveraged gambling.

Peddling Your Wares Through the Interest Rate Cycle

- Countrywide Financial goes to the school of hard knocks and graduates with a "macro hedging" degree. Its "natural business hedge" deftly balances its risks in the mortgage lending and servicing markets.
- Washington Mutual illustrates how the best-laid hedging plans sometimes go astray—when the executive team finds itself stretched beyond its own organizational capabilities.

"The Federal Reserve bumped up interest rates yesterday by a bold half point, pushing a key rate to its highest level in nine years. Fed policymakers signaled they were prepared to move even more aggressively if needed to fight inflation ...

The Fed's action at mid-afternoon was immediately matched by announcements from commercial banks that they were increasing their prime lending rate—the benchmark for millions of consumer and business loans—by the same half point."

—Associated Press

Just as there is a business cycle that goes up in expansions and down in recessions, and just as there are wave-like bullish and bearish moves in the stock market, so, too, is there a very well-defined *interest rate cycle.*

Over time, interest rates will move up when lifted by concerns over inflationary pressures and the raising of short-term interest rates by the Federal Reserve. At some point, however, if the Fed raises interest rates too swiftly, it will choke off the economy and cause a recession. At this point, interest rates tend to fall with associated deflationary pressures.

Being able to profitably peddle one's wares through these often gut-wrenching ups and downs of the interest rate cycle is one of the biggest challenges many interest rate-sensitive companies face. This is particularly true of two of the biggest mortgage lenders in the game: Countrywide Financial and Washington Mutual.

With Countrywide, we will see a company that has constructed a brilliant "natural business hedge" that deftly balances its mortgage-origination and mortgage-servicing businesses and thereby protects the company through *all* phases of the interest rate cycle. By way of cautionary contrast, Washington Mutual offers a great example of how an executive team might talk a very good hedging game. However, we will also see how its best-laid hedging plans have at least sometimes gone seriously astray because of poor strategic execution.

Countrywide Deploys a School of Hard Knocks "Macro Hedge"

"Loan origination (or production) performs well when interest rates are low and falling as borrowers seek to refinance existing mortgages, so volume and margins are higher. Conversely, loan servicing performs well when interest rates are high and rising because lower refinance volume means income from the servicing business is larger and more stable. When properly managed and balanced, however, they form a natural hedge which is designed to allow Countrywide to produce a stable and growing income stream."

—**Countrywide Financial Glossary**

Countrywide Financial is the largest independent residential mortgage lending company in the United States At this point in its history, it is also highly successful—but this was not always so. In fact, Countrywide had to learn how to hedge its interest rate risk at the worst possible time and in the hardest of ways.

To understand why, we need to go back to 1969—the year Countrywide was founded. This was the year Neil Armstrong took "one small step for man" and "one giant leap for mankind." But it was also on the eve of one of the most turbulent interest rate cycles in history, when mortgage rates rocketed through the 10 percent barrier like Apollo 11 on its way to the moon.

Back then, the company was named Countrywide Credit Industries, and its main line of business was residential mortgage banking. Rocked by the interest rate volatility that would characterize both the 1970s and 1980s, Countrywide developed its macroeconomic hedging strategy as a matter of pure survival.

This strategy is predicated on the countercyclical nature of two of its major business units—*loan origination* and *loan servicing*. At one end of the macro hedge, Countrywide Home Loans business unit generates revenue on its loan production, which *increases* as interest rates *decline*. At the other end of the macro hedge, the company's Mortgage Servicing Rights business sees its profits increase when interest rates *increase.*

As noted in the preceding excerpt from Countrywide's Financial Glossary, this inverse relationship between loan production and loan servicing serves as a natural business hedge against interest rate risk. As a further revenue anchor to this relationship, Countrywide also traffics in noncyclical insurance products. That this strategy has been highly effective is evident in what has become an almost routine type of announcement from Countrywide's Master Cyclist CEO, Angelo Mozilo:

> *Countrywide has delivered exceptional third quarter results, establishing a new milestone in the company's earnings history. ... Our versatile macro-hedge strategy empowered the company to maximize opportunities presented by the refinance boom. The company set a new quarterly record for net earnings of $161 million.*

WaMu's Gang That Couldn't Hedge Straight

> *"By skillful hedging, lenders like Countrywide, Wells Fargo, and Fannie Mae are able to smooth earnings through interest-rate cycles, producing strong profits even in periods of tight money like the one we seem to be entering. But WaMu's hedging, at least so far, hasn't worked that way."*
>
> **—Shawn Tully,** *Fortune*

Washington Mutual is particularly interesting because it illustrates how a CEO who seemed savvy about interest rate cycles—but who was all too hyperkinetic—wound up hoisted on his own hedging petard.

When CEO Kerry Killinger first joined "WaMu" in 1982, it was a small Seattle-based thrift highly vulnerable both to the cyclical vagaries of the regional economy and the large interest rate risks typically borne by thrift institutions. Today, the company has evolved into the largest thrift institution in the United States

From almost the very beginning, Killinger and his executive team were determined to cure Washington Mutual once and for all of the dreaded "thrift disease"—a chronically depressed stock price brought on by a typical thrift institution's higher costs of funds and massive exposure to interest rate risk.

To understand the problem—and Killinger's proposed cure—it is useful to understand how traditional thrift institutions typically turn a profit and why they are heavily exposed to so-called "spread risk." Such thrifts borrow money at short-term interest rates, repackage the funds at higher long-term rates as home mortgages, and earn their profits on the "spread" between short- and long-term rates. However, spread risk manifests itself every time the Federal Reserve starts raising short-term interest rates to slow down the economy and fight inflation. This narrows the spread and can severely squeeze the thrift's profits on spread income.

In the worst-case scenario—one that can make a thrift institution CEO wake up in a cold sweat—the Fed can raise rates so high that short-term interest rates rise *above* long-term rates. In such cases, thrifts actually lose money on their mortgage portfolio— sometimes *lots* of money.

To combat such spread risk—and various other risks associated with the interest rate cycle—Killinger and his executive team set out to develop a "balanced business model"—one in which, as the preceding excerpt relates, "countervailing forces" would allow WaMu to be "successful in all parts of the cycle."

At least part of this balanced business model looks a lot like the natural business hedge that Countrywide Financial has constructed. Like Countrywide, WaMu has sought to be a market leader in both loan originations, which increase as interest rates fall, and loan servicing, the revenues of which increase as interest rates rise.

In addition, WaMu has adopted an interesting risk-management approach with respect to its issuance of fixed-rate versus adjustable-rate mortgages. Because fixed-rate mortgages are far more vulnerable to spread risk, WaMu immediately resells them into the secondary market upon origination, *but* it retains the servicing rights to them. In contrast, WaMu holds on to its adjustable-rate mortgage originations to earn interest income on them *and* services them, too.

In principle, then, WaMu seems to have covered its bases. In practice, however, these best-laid hedging plans have, at times, gone wildly astray. Indeed, in just a single quarter after interest rates began to rise in 2004, WaMu managed to lose billions on its hedges! That WaMu's natural business hedge failed to deliver for WaMu is evident in this stinging rebuke from *Fortune* magazine:

> *As expected, rising [interest] rates had indeed caused a big increase in the value of the servicing business: $1.7bn. That should have been enough to cover WaMu's hedging costs and still contribute money to the bank's bottom line. But amazingly, hedging had generated a $2.4 billion loss. It totally wiped out the servicing gain, as well as the bank's income from originations, leaving WaMu with a $63m loss from mortgage banking.*

As to what exactly went wrong at WaMu, the company failed to properly execute the most important part of its hedging strategy. As discussed much more in the next chapter on business unit diversification, this was to transform itself from a mortgage-dependent thrift into a broadly diversified financial services group.

Instead, WaMu's acquisition-happy CEO continued his frenetic buying binge of mortgage lenders well into the late stages of the bottoming of the interest rate cycle. Of course, when that interest rate cycle turned inexorably back up—as it always does—WaMu still found itself with a bad case of thrift disease. Countrywide's Mozilo later described this gang that could not hedge straight: "WaMu was touted as a world beater.... But it grew too fast. It didn't have the organizational or intellectual capacity to run a business of that size."

▪▪▪ Key Points

▪ **Hedging Commodity Price, Interest Rate, and Exchange Rate Risks**

- Companies face specific macroeconomic risks that range from oil price shocks and interest rate spikes to movements in commodity prices and exchange rates.

- The failure to hedge these specific macroeconomic risks is a *de facto* "do-nothing" strategy that can lead to major losses.

- Financial derivatives such as futures and options as well as natural business hedges can be used to mitigate these risks.

▪ **Strategic Versus Tactical Hedging**

- Master Cyclist executive teams employ sophisticated economic forecasting tools and equally sophisticated analyses of industry conditions to guide their hedging strategies and tactics.

- Strategic hedging completely hedges a particular kind of risk and allows a company to focus on its core competency.

- Tactical hedging—the true mark of the Master Cyclist—entails proactively and opportunistically adjusting the level of a hedge in anticipation of future conditions (for example, a forecast increase in oil prices).

▪ **Exchange Rate Risk and the Incredibly Shrinking Dollar**

- Translation risk describes the effect of converting a currency such as the euro earned abroad into dollars.

- Transaction risk arises when a company commits to purchasing foreign goods with the domestic currency at some future point in time.

Peddling Risk Free Through the Interest Rate Cycle

- Spread risk manifests itself when short-term rates rise relative to long-term rates. This squeezes the spread between short- and long-term rates that financial institutions normally earn when they borrow loanable funds at short-term rates and lend them at longer-term rates.

9

When You Can't Beat the Business Cycle, Hedge Its Risks!

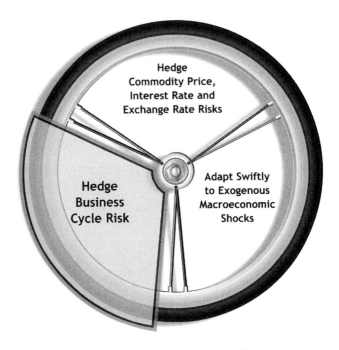

"Breaking away from being captive of domestic economic cycles is the thing we've been working on for the last six years. We've done that by geographic and market diversity, rather than product diversity. We've gone to more countries. We've gone to more customers in different industries."
—Kenneth Butterworth, Chairman and CEO, Loctite Corporation

Much the work of the Master Cyclist executive team is devoted to first forecasting and anticipating movements in the business cycle and then implementing proactive strategies and tactics to take advantage of the opportunities that such movements present. As we have seen, for example, the Master Cyclist team will begin to cut back on production, trim inventories, and ratchet down capital expenditures in anticipation of a recession; whereas during a recession, the team might "cherry pick" from a swollen labor force to get top talent at bargain wages.

This is hardly the whole story, however—at least when it comes to managing general business cycle risk. This is because the Master Cyclist team also knows that even if its forecasts are 70 percent accurate, the other 30 percent of wrong predictions can bankrupt you.

For this reason, Master Cyclist strategists often also seek to hedge at least some of that business cycle risk. The tools most useful in this task range from *business unit diversification* and *geographical diversification* to the *outsourcing* and *offshoring* of different elements of the manufacturing and supply chain.

Business Unit Diversification

- While a myopic Hewlett Packard sinks deeper into the computer hardware cyclical muck, IBM daringly escapes by diversifying into services, Web hosting, and strategic outsourcing.
- Always dominant in the air-delivery skies, FedEx and its strategic pilots execute a highly successful ground-transportation blitzkrieg against rival UPS.

"The challenge is not to avoid business cycles but to manage in such a way that [the business units will] perform, on average, well. In my opinion, [it] is next to impossible to be in the chemical industry and to avoid cyclicity. Steady income from the gas business, pharmaceuticals, and vitamins should help BASF."

—Jurgen Strube, CEO, BASF

A lot of good synergistic and strategic reasons that might lead a company to diversify have *nothing* to do with managing business cycle risk and broader macroeconomic risk. For example, an automaker that also begins to produce light trucks might be able to build larger manufacturing facilities and thereby realize *"economies of scale"* and lower unit costs. At the same time, if parts or assemblies can be used in *both* cars and light trucks—chasses, shocks, brake drums, or engines—the vehicle maker can also realize *"economies of scope"* by jointly producing the two kinds of vehicles that produce similar cost savings.

More broadly, many other strategic reasons to diversify have little or no risk-hedging motives. In this regard, business units within a company that can share markets or distribution systems or a common process or technology can all benefit from *synergies* that can help their company outperform a rival that focuses more narrowly on a single product or service.

That said, there are equally obvious risk-hedging benefits to various forms of business unit diversification. You saw, for example, with Countrywide Financial in the preceding chapter, how it has created a natural business model hedge by having one business unit that focuses on mortgage loan originations and another that focuses on mortgage loan servicing. That example showed how these two businesses are "negatively correlated" with movements in interest rates. That is, when the revenues of one unit rise with a change in interest rates, the revenues of the other unit tend to fall. The result is that Countrywide can achieve more stable revenues over the course of the business cycle and related interest rate cycle.

With the contrasting examples of Hewlett-Packard and IBM that now follow, you will see how two technology giants both sought at one critical juncture to strategically diversify to avoid the extreme cyclicity of the computer hardware industry. But you will also see how the abject failure of HP to successfully execute its diversification strategy both led to its fall from shareholder grace *and* gave a huge, albeit unintended, boost to IBM's diversification efforts.

HP's Diversification Road Not Taken and Fiorina's Folly

"While most analysts see the Compaq acquisition as the defining moment of [CEO Carly] Fiorina's HP tenure, another deal that didn't happen was almost as important. That was HP's failed attempt to acquire PricewaterhouseCoopers in 2000, which would have created a larger army of consultants with which to challenge IBM Global Services. The deal fell apart, and IBM acquired PWC two years later. 'In the end that took them out of the capability to challenge IBM Global Services....'"

—B to B Magazine

Hewlett-Packard is the second largest computer maker in the world and a premier player in the much higher-margin world of printers. It is also a company that came to a very important fork in the road at the turn of the century and wound up taking a very wrong turn.

HP's CEO at the time was Carly Fiorina, and she came within $18 billion of almost getting it right. The $18 billion was the offer she made in November 2000 for the 30,000-strong army of consultants that comprised the consulting wing of PricewaterhouseCoopers (PWC).

Sure, it was an overinflated price made at the height of the dot.com boom. But at least Fiorina's vision was right. She seemed to understand, at least at that point, that there were two basic problems with heavily relying on the personal computer and printer business.

One problem is the sector's extreme vulnerability to business cycle downturns. The second, more subtle, problem is that both personal computers and printers were, at that time, becoming more and more like commodities sold at low margins—hardly a business you want to be in to ensure double-digit annual growth rates.

Fiorina's solution was to follow IBM into the IT consulting services area, and the PricewaterhouseCoopers acquisition would be HP's entrée into this lucrative market. In fact, from a Master Cyclist viewpoint, diversifying into services would have several advantages.

IT consulting is, in many ways, a countercyclical business that provides a natural business hedge to the ups and downs of the PC world. This is not just because the services industry is more stable. It is also because as the economy turns down, the demand for cost-cutting solutions such as improved supply chain management and outsourcing go up.

In addition, by having a consulting presence higher up in the retail chain, HP's consulting capabilities would allow it to package more product to customers, particularly in the high-end and high-margin server market.

Note, however, that Fiorina's vision of a natural-hedged HP came crashing down just one month after her bold bid for PWC. This was when a perfectly abysmal quarterly earnings report shaved 15 percent off HP's stock price in a single day and made the already rich bid for PWC too much for HP to handle. What would happen the following year would be as inexplicable as it was ill advised.

Indeed, Fiorina staked her reputation and company on following a highly *un*diversified path as HP acquired Compaq and tried to establish its preeminence in the highly cyclical and maturing PC business. This dive deeper into the cyclical muck only served to antagonize HP's major rival, Dell.

With its leaner, more efficient business model, Dell's aggressive pricing not only hammered HP's margins. Dell also redoubled its efforts to break HP's strong hold on the printer market. The result was, of course, Fiorina's undiversified folly.

As to what eventually happened to PWC, it became (ironically), as the next example shows, the crown jewel in IBM's highly successful diversification strategy.

IBM Does a "Robert Frost" on HP's Road Not Taken

"Two roads diverged in a wood, and I—
I took the one less traveled by,
And that has made all the difference."
            —Robert Frost

"Whether or not there is a softening of the economy [in
2001], IBM should be in reasonably good competitive
shape. Of course, we all hope such a downturn
doesn't occur. But if it does, the ebbing tide may not
beach all boats. For one thing, service offerings like
outsourcing and hosting are cost saving propositions
for our customers. Services, in this regard, is a
counter-cyclical business."
            —IBM 2000 Annual Report

This second excerpt provides an exclamation point to IBM's successful transformation from a big mainframe-dependent elephant under siege from the Dells and Gateways of the personal computer revolution into a naturally hedged and very nimble IT services behemoth. What is so impressive about this is that Big Blue's Master Cyclists saw the need for this hedging long before the 2001 recession actually occurred and well prior to the bursting of the tech bubble.

This transformation began in 1996 with the formation of IBM Global Services. By the 2001 recession, that transformation was almost complete because IBM would get more revenue from strategic outsourcing and services than its vaunted hardware.

One year later, IBM acquired PWC—the acquisitions equivalent of the "Great Train Robbery." It wasn't just that this acquisition added 30,000 additional highly trained individuals to its existing army of 150,000 consultants and brought IBM shoulder to shoulder with the industry leader Accenture. It is also that the price of $3.5 billion was a small fraction of what rival HP had offered just two years earlier.

In fact, this acquisition thematically illustrates the same kind of patience and analytical awareness we observed in an earlier chapter with Fair Isaac's acquisition of HNC Software. IBM saw a chessboard in which the stock market had collapsed and the value of PWC had plummeted. In addition, in the wake of the Enron scandal, accounting firms like PricewaterhouseCoopers were under regulatory pressure to divest their consulting wings, so the company was an all-too-eager seller. That IBM was able to use the currency of its own stock for most of the bargain-basement price was just icing on a cake that one analyst described as "the smartest move they've made in 10 years."

As a final coda to this example, it is perhaps also worth mentioning that in 2005—the same year that Carly Fiorina got fired for dragging HP further into the cyclical muck of the PC market with her Compaq gambit—IBM also sold off its entire PC business to the Chinese company Lenovo and finally left behind the cyclicity and commodization of that business forever.

FedEx Takes to the Ground to Strategically Diversify

"Thanks to diversification and coordination among its business units, FedEx has been able to shift resources during the recent economic downturn. … In many cases, FedEx has been able to divert overnight business to its cheaper ground shipment business. Before it had that option, FedEx would lose those customers to rival United Parcel Service, Inc."

—Investor's Business Daily

Recall that in Chapter 4, "The Art of 'Cherry Picking' and Other Well-Timed Tactics of the Human Resources Manager," the point was made that a "no-layoffs" policy is likely to be doomed to failure unless it is accompanied by sound Master Cyclist management. This next example of Federal Express' business unit diversification strategy helps further illustrate the company's sophisticated understanding of business cycle risk.

During the early days of FedEx, such business cycle risk was extremely high as the company depended entirely on airborne express delivery. However, over time, FedEx's executive team learned a very important lesson: *There is a critical complementary relationship between the air-delivery and ground-delivery markets.*

In particular, during good times, the air-delivery markets tends to outperform; when the economy softens, companies move more toward ground delivery to save money. In practical terms, this meant that whenever the economy would soften, the hitherto undiversified FedEx would lose market share to its archrival and ground-transportation dominant player United Parcel Service.

FedEx's diversification into ground transportation would, however, kick into high gear in 1997. That's when the company shelled out $2.7 billion to acquire Caliber Technologies—one of UPS's main competitors in the ground service market. This marked a major milestone in what has come to be the broader war between FedEx and UPS over the "package-delivery market" and a now more broadly defined set of supply chain management services that connect customers to the global marketplace.

Following that key acquisition, FedEx invested heavily in upgrading its ground-service technology and creating a network that can easily help its customers move away from higher-priced services such as overnight delivery into less-expensive alternatives when economic conditions warrant. In addition, the 2004 acquisition of Kinko's boosted FedEx's retail presence and proved to be an important counterpoint to the chain of UPS stores.

More broadly, FedEx also has reorganized its operations in a way that makes it essentially a one-stop shop for customers. This reorganization involved the establishment of units that can handle overnight air shipments, ground delivery, regional freight, customs, and other services. As Alan Graf, the CFO of FedEx succinctly put it in the wake of the 2001 recession, "All of those [steps] have been vital in helping us withstand this current economic malaise."[1]

▪▪▪ Geographical Diversification

- ▪ Using a mastery of the intricacies of exchange rates learned from an earlier peso crisis, the Mexican cement magnate CEMEX tactically advances its geographical diversification strategy during the Asian currency meltdown.

"Geographic diversification enables us to operate in multiple regions with different business cycles. For the long term, we are trying to ensure that no one market accounts for more than a third of our business."
—Lorenzo Zambrano, Chairman of the Board and CEO, CEMEX

As with business unit diversification, many compelling strategic reasons to geographically diversify likewise have nothing to do with the hedging of business cycle risk. By diversifying into new foreign markets, companies can achieve greater economies of scale. They can also deploy their core managerial and production skills across a broader range of opportunities.

These kinds of strategic benefits notwithstanding, it is also true that one of the primary benefits of geographical diversification is to significantly reduce business cycle risk. The reason that geographical diversification can be so effective is that, as a matter of statistical truth, the business cycles and political conditions of various countries are not "perfectly correlated" statistically. In lay terms, this means that while Europe or Japan might be experiencing a recession, China or the United States might be in the midst of a robust expansion.

More subtly, it is also true that the business cycles of developing countries such as China and India and Vietnam and Brazil tend to be far less correlated with the business cycles of developed countries such as Canada, the United States, and France. For this reason, "multinational companies" that might be based in developed nations view developing nations not just as new and untapped markets but also as excellent risk-hedging destinations.

Of course, this is not to say that a recession in one country such as Japan or one continent such as Europe cannot spread to other countries and regions. In what is now an almost seamless global economy, there are significant "transmission effects" across countries and regions. Still, there remain important opportunities to geographically diversify for risk-hedging purposes.

This is a lesson we can learn well from the globally diversified cement magnate CEMEX—even as we see an incredibly well-executed tactical gambit involving the opportunistic leveraging of exchange rate risk.

CEMEX Grabs the Asian Tiger by the Exchange Rate Tail

"Our best opportunities have come at the worst times.…
We need to be in many markets to survive."
—Lorenzo Zambrano, Chairman of the Board
and CEO, CEMEX

Mexico has had few companies as successful as CEMEX. This is a company that traces its origins all the way back to 1906. However, it wasn't until 1992, with the acquisition of the two main cement companies in Spain, that CEMEX became a truly multinational company.

Since that time, CEMEX's aggressive geographic diversification acquisition strategy "to be in many markets to survive" has propelled it to its position of third-largest cement producer in the world—behind only Holcim of Switzerland and Lafarge of France. In fact, this is a geographical diversification strategy that has often been well timed to the global business cycle by its visionary CEO, Lorenzo Zambrano.

Consider for example, CEMEX's bold tactical gambit during the Asian financial crisis of 1997–1998. The devaluation of the Thai baht not only triggered a chain reaction of plunging currency values across Asia. It also resulted in a plunge in regional stock indices.

Prior to these events, CEMEX had long had its eye on a key strategic acquisition in the Philippines.

When the Philippine peso plunged—and took the Philippine stock market down with it—Zambrano's CEMEX scooped up 30 percent of Rizal Cement company for a mere $93 million. Zambrano then followed that acquisition up with the purchase of another 40 percent of Rizal.

CEMEX did not stop in the Philippines, however. It also grabbed 25 percent of Indonesia's largest cement producer, PT Semen Gresik, at an attractive price.

There is at least one other very interesting subplot in the CEMEX story. It has to do with how Zambrano had the sound macroeconomic sense to execute his global diversification strategy during these turbulent times.

In this regard, the devaluing of the Mexican peso in 1994 and the resulting severe economic crisis in Mexico in 1995 had given Zambrano a very bitter taste of what can happen to a company's stock price when the local currency begins to fall dramatically. During that time, CEMEX's stock price fell, as did the valuation of the company—to a point arguably well below its value. Although CEMEX fought back quickly from the peso crisis and the company's undervalued position, Zambrano no doubt understood better than most executives how valuations can get significantly out of whack during currency crises and thereby create incredible buying opportunities.

▪▪▪ Outsourcing and Offshoring Risk

- A cross-town battle between Broadcom's chess players and Conexant's confederacy of dunces illustrates the virtues of outsourcing high-risk manufacturing while embracing high-value-added component design and distribution.
- Affiliated Computer Services rides the outsourcing wave—offering sophisticated offshoring solutions in its own broadly diversified manner.

"Outsourcing ... can be cheaper and offer the organization more specialized knowledge, but can you trust it?"

—Carl Weinschenk,
TechRepublic.com

Outsourcing refers to work done for one company by another or work done by people other than the company's full-time employees. Such outsourcing can be done domestically within a company's own country or, alternatively, the outsourcing can move "offshore" to other countries.

Although outsourcing and offshoring might help to reduce the business cycle risk of maintaining a workforce to provide an element of a company's business—anything from data processing, security, and marketing to the manufacture of subassemblies or the provision of delivery systems—these strategies are not without their own risks.

For example, it might not always be wise to outsource a "mission-critical" subassembly or procedure to an outside group. This is particular true if the procedure or subassembly has been offshored to a country where there might be political or economic instability, where there is a lack of skilled workers and expertise, or even when there is a cultural mismatch with the offshoring partner.

Moreover, even though a company might save on labor costs during a recession, that same company might be exposed to a significant increase in outsourcing costs in a rapidly expanding economy if the company has not locked in prices in longer-term contracts in a timely way.

That said, many companies nonetheless find outsourcing and offshoring to be valuable strategies in the reduction of business cycle risk.

Broadcom's Two-Pronged Diversification and Outsourcing Strategy

"We are at once a company focused entirely on broadband solutions, and yet a company that provides a diverse portfolio of products targeted to a number of different broadband communications markets. That diversity provided us a level of stability not enjoyed by companies focused on a single market. Additionally, we saw further and dramatic validation of our fabless manufacturing model, which allows us to keep capital expenditures low. The model was especially beneficial during the weak economic period.
—**Henry Nicholas and Henry Samueli, co-chairmen, Broadcom**

Broadcom and its "cross-town rival" Conexant (first introduced in Chapter 5, "'Macromanaging' Your Production, Inventory, and Supply Chain") are located within just a few miles from one another and very close to my UC-Irvine business school campus. In honor of its own name, Broadcom's specialty is in the area of broadband communications, and the company's ambition is to "own" the high-speed networks of the future by supplying chips to all its critical parts. Toward this end, the company makes highly sophisticated chips called "integrated circuits" that can be used in a variety of broadband applications—from digital set-top boxes and cable modems for the home TV market to DSL lines, wireless applications, servers, and other networking "gear."

In the late 1990s, Broadcom's executive team adopted a two-pronged strategy that quickly differentiated it from its neighbor and competitor Conexant. One prong of the strategy involved a conscious effort to diversify its product line across all elements of the broadband supply and product chains. Broadcom did this through a very ambitious acquisition program. However, unlike Conexant, which encumbered itself with debt, Broadcom cleverly financed with the currency of its own high-priced stock.

The second prong of Broadcom's strategy involved outsourcing all of its chip fabrication needs. In this "fabless" model, instead of insisting on manufacturing its own chips, Broadcom chose to focus solely on the higher-value-added *design* end of the business and offshored its production to chip "foundries" or "fabs" located primarily in Southeast Asia.

The excerpt leading off this example from Broadcom's dynamic executive duo of Nicholas and Samueli from the company's 2001 Annual Report provides strong testimony to the effectiveness of this two-pronged narrow-diversification and outsourcing strategy. During the technology crash of 2001, it was not Broadcom left holding the huge inventory stockpiles, but rather customers such as Hewlett-Packard, Motorola, and Cisco. Over time, Broadcom has continued to increase its revenues and stock price while the "incredibly shrinking Conexant" has fallen by the penny-stock wayside.

Conexant's Confederacy of Not So *Fab*ulous Dunces

"Conexant is a fabless semiconductor company with approximately 1,400 employees worldwide."
—**Conexant 2003 Annual Report**

Just three years before, Conexant's executive team had boasted in an earlier Annual Report that it owned its own chip "fab" and employed almost 9,000 people. How Conexant devolved from a fab-driven company into a "fabless" former shell of itself with 1,400 employees and penny-stock status is a cautionary tale for any would-be Reactive Cyclist who chooses to ignore the risks of the business cycle.

In fact, the company's downfall began with the initial decision of the executive team *not* to outsource much of its chip manufacturing. In this regard, the semiconductor industry is infamous for its volatile swings; and through the often wildly swinging industry cycles, invariably it is the large fabrication plants or "fabs" that bear the brunt of periodic chip gluts and plunging prices. Moreover, chip fabrication is a process characterized by large economies of scale and rapid technological change, so that the only way to be competitive in the market is to always be the biggest and most modern fab on the block.

So it was that within a year of its 1999 spinoff from Rockwell, the relatively small Conexant found itself playing well over its head with the really big boys—huge Taiwanese fabs such as Taiwan Semiconductor and United Microelectronics that feed companies such as Phillips and Motorola with their chips. In this fast-moving chip arena, Conexant belatedly realized the errors of its nonoutsourcing ways, that its level of capital expenditures was insufficient to stay on the leading edge of chip production.

At this painful point, the company made the decision to realign its strategy and go, like Broadcom, to a "fabless," outsourcing model. However, in executing this new strategy, Conexant stumbled further.

The dilemma the company faced was its belief that it had developed a very important specialty process technology involving silicon germanium, or so-called SiGe, chips. Its fear was that if it sold off its fab, it might not be able to retain and further develop its SiGe process technologies.

As a result of temporizing over this dilemma, Conexant lost any opportunity to sell off its fab at a decent price near the top of the semiconductor market. Instead, it wound up almost giving away 55 percent of this fab to the Carlyle Group for pennies on the dollar.

ACS Surfs the Outsourcing and Offshoring Tsunami

"Record revenue, record profits, record net income, record earnings per share, record new business signings, and record cash flow all combined for a remarkable year for ACS."

—**ACS 2002 Annual Report**

Affiliated Computer Services is interesting because it illustrates the other end of both the outsourcing and offshoring markets. Given its strategic positioning as an outsourcing provider, ACS has been able to skillfully ride the tsunami of a powerful global trend.

Because of this positioning, ACS was able to do in treacherous recessionary times what most companies in the United States only dreamed about: generate large profits, earnings, and cash flow while the economy was still suffering.

Before getting into the details of this example, I want to reiterate the point that the hedging or reduction of business cycle risk is not the only reason—and might not even be the most important reason—that many companies outsource. In the increasingly sophisticated worlds of both supply chain management and management strategy, it is now well understood that outsourcing can be a very useful *micro*management tool irrespective of movements in the business cycle.

For example, by allowing more efficient companies such as ACS to handle certain functions such as data processing and "back-office" paperwork, outsourcing can reduce costs along the supply chain even as it allows many companies from a strategic perspective to focus on their own "core competencies." That said, it is equally true that the 2001 recession was a macromanaging epiphany for the executive teams of many companies in that it underscored the value of outsourcing particular cycle-sensitive functions to specifically reduce one's exposure to business cycle and macroeconomic risk.

It is within the context of these micro- and macromanagement observations that ACS grew with astonishing speed over the course of a decade to become one of the largest providers of outsourcing services—one that generates more than $4 billion in revenue per year. Still and all, *what is perhaps most interesting— and admirable—about ACS is its sophisticated understanding of the need for the company to engage in its own business cycle hedging strategies.*

In this regard, in the same spirit as Broadcom, Countrywide, and IBM, ACS has built a very balanced portfolio of outsourcing and offshoring services that are diversified both at the business unit and geographical levels. This portfolio not only includes "technology outsourcing"—the company offers Web programmers, system analysts, and network engineers. It also includes the largest part of its business: business process outsourcing.

In this area, the company handles many of the front- and back-office functions of myriad companies—from billing, call centers, and customer service to the processing of health-care claims, loan applications, and documents. *By cutting across such a wide swath of industry sectors, ACS builds its own hedge!*

In addition, as a matter of strategy, ACS has also aggressively diversified into the provision of outsourcing services for local, state, and federal government. Yes, it has done so to take advantage of a trend that began in the 1990s to "reinvent government"—conservative code for privatizing many of the functions of government. However, this diversification strategy clearly also helps ACS reduce its own business cycle risk—because government business is far less prone to the vagaries of the business cycle.

Today, as a result of this diversification, ACS handles nearly half of the nation's Medicaid claims, manages more than half a million desktop computers for NASA, and provides virtual city halls and constituency-relationship management systems for big states such as Texas and New York and smaller states such as Oregon and Wyoming.

The result of all of this is that ACS was able to put together an impressive string of banner years going back to the 2001 recession—even as many other companies during that time experienced either stagnant or negative growth.

▬▬■ Key Points

- ■ **Business Cycle Hedging Strategies**
  - Because economic forecasting is not 100 percent accurate, Master Cyclist strategists often seek to hedge at least some business cycle risk.
  - Effective hedging strategies include business unit and geographical diversification as well as outsourcing and offshoring.
- ■ **Business Unit Diversification**
  - Companies engage in business unit diversification for many reasons other than to hedge business cycle risk—from achieving greater economies of scale and scope to capturing the synergies that result from sharing markets, distribution systems, or processes.
  - However, business unit diversification can also be used to construct natural business hedges to achieve more stable earnings over the course of the business cycle.
  - Two business units are naturally hedged if their activities are *negatively correlated* over the business cycle.
- ■ **Geographical Diversification**
  - By geographically diversifying into new countries and regions, companies can achieve greater economies of scale while deploying their core managerial and production skills across a broader range of opportunities.
  - Nonetheless, the greatest benefit of geographical diversification is often the hedge it provides against business cycle risk.

- The effectiveness of geographical diversification as a hedge is rooted in the fact that business cycles and political conditions of various countries are not perfectly correlated.

- Because the business cycles of *developing* countries such as China or Brazil tend to be less correlated with the business cycles of *developed* countries such as Canada or France, "multinational companies" view developing nations as excellent risk-hedging destinations.

Outsourcing and Offshoring Your Risk

- Outsourcing refers to work done for a company by another company or by people other than the company's full-time employees.

- Offshoring refers to work outsourced to other countries.

- By selectively outsourcing and offshoring non-mission-critical elements, a company can help reduce its business cycle risk.

10

Surviving—and Prospering from—the Economic Shocks of War, Terrorism, Drought, and Disease

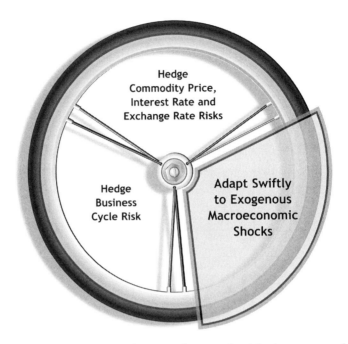

"*When written in Chinese, the word* crisis *is composed of two characters. One represents danger. The other represents opportunity.*"

—**John F. Kennedy**

A new kind of dangerous mountain warfare in Afghanistan and an ugly form of close urban combat in Iraq create lucrative opportunities for companies such as General Atomics to sell its high-altitude spy drones, Flir to move its infrared goggles, and Ceradyne to hawk its ceramic body armor.

Terrorism sparks a boom in products as diverse as bomb-detection equipment and biometric identification, and companies such as InVision and Viisage prosper while bird flu sweeping across Asia sets off a vaccine-development sweepstakes to the benefit of large companies such as MedImmune and small speculative ventures such as China's Sinovac. Is it any wonder that economics has been dubbed the "dismal science"?

Dismal and grim though these thoughts might be, neither the dangers *nor* the opportunities that arise from random macroeconomic shocks should be ignored by any "big-picture" executive team seeking to protect and expand shareholder value. And here's the key point: Random macroeconomic shocks are, by very definition, random. However, their after-effects are often quite logical and therefore often possible to anticipate and exploit.

Unfortunately, in the chaos that often ensues after a random shock, many executive teams are caught flat-footed. Master Cyclist executive teams are, however, immediately able to parse both the tactical implications of a random shock as well as their possible longer-term strategic opportunities. These are just some of their stories.

War and Terrorism

- Casino kingpin Caesar's immediately retargets its market in the aftermath of 9/11, tactically shifting from national and international air travelers to gamblers within easy driving distance in Southern California and the region.
- Southwest Airlines builds goodwill—and market share!—by immediately cutting prices and offering penalty-free cancellations post 9/11 while other carriers like the hapless United adopt a de facto "tough-luck" policy.

> *"'Exogenous shock,' the term that economists use for events from outside the economy but that affect economic activity, has a grim redundancy when applied to the Sept. 11, 2001, attacks on the N.Y. World Trade Center and Pentagon. The term literally means 'a blow from outside the system'—like a fuel-laden jetliner crashing into a skyscraper."*
> **—Edward Lotterman, Bismarck Tribune**

The 9/11 terrorist attacks caught an entire world by surprise. However, many of the economic adjustments that followed turned out to be quite logical—if only an executive team was skilled enough to foresee them. The swift tactical responses of Caesar's and Southwest Airlines offer two important lessons in marketing through such extreme economic turbulence.

Caesar's Grounds Its Marketing Campaign

> *"Gambling is in some ways a recession-proof industry—people will gamble even when they can't afford it—but even high rollers can't quite ignore the fear of terrorism, which made people less inclined to travel to Vegas and other gambling hot spots after the Sept. 11 attacks."*
>
> **—CNNMoney.com**

Even before becoming part of the Harrah's empire in 2005, Caesar's Entertainment was one of the world's largest gaming companies. Headquartered in Las Vegas, it runs about 30 resorts around the world, including notable brands such as Caesar's Palace, Ballys, and Paris Las Vegas, and generates close to $5 billion in revenues annually.

The company's rapid response to the events of 9/11 illustrates how Caesar's executive team immediately grasped the consequences of 9/11 for the gaming industry—and then reacted both swiftly and decisively. For starters, the company immediately canceled a major $500 million capital expenditure—the building of a new 900-suite tower at its premier Caesar's Palace Resort.

Within a week of the attacks, the company also laid off 5 percent of its workforce and cut hours for many more. To squeeze its supply chain and creditors, the company then used its large size and this time of extreme uncertainty to renegotiate many of its financial covenants.

By far, the most interesting and subtle response to 9/11 came when the company quickly and tactically shifted its marketing emphasis. Rather than continue to advertise heavily to its traditional customer core—air travelers flying in from all over the nation and the globe—Caesar's quickly refocused on the large Southern California and other nearby regional markets that were within easy driving distance.

As a result of these proactive measures, the company was not only able to cut its losses in the short run. By the fourth quarter of 2001, Caesar's actually increased its revenues over the fourth quarter of 2000.

Southwest Airlines Builds Goodwill in the Wake of 9/11

> *"I encourage people to fly again but at the same time, at Southwest, we are known for our customer service, and we always want to do the right thing for our customers."*
>
> **—Kristen Nelson, company spokeswoman,**
> **Southwest Airlines**

In an earlier chapter, we saw Southwest fly circles around its competition with regards to fuel price hedging. The incredibly swift tactical response of its executive team to 9/11 likewise earns the company kudos in the marketing department.

On the *very day* of the 9/11 attack, the customer service-oriented Southwest announced that any passenger with a confirmed reservation could request a full refund *regardless* of the travel date. The company also maintained a full schedule of flights and had no employee layoffs. In addition, on both September 21 and 24, the company significantly cut its fares. It furthermore waived any and all penalty fees associated with rebooking flights.

In contrast, most other carriers—from American and Continental to Delta and United—practiced a "tough-luck" policy in which refunds were limited to a very short time interval—typically one to two weeks after the attack. These other carriers were also much slower to institute price cuts, and many drastically cut their schedules even as they instituted massive layoffs.

For Southwest, the result of its expressions of goodwill, its nimble marketing and pricing strategy, and its projection of an air of confidence in maintaining its schedule and workforce was a powerful one—an increase in market share with a more loyal customer base. Perhaps not coincidentally, Southwest's stock price steadily rebounded after 9/11, and the company actually turned a profit in 2001.

Oil Price Shocks

- Progressive's "chess players" perfectly execute an ingenious oil price shock tactical gambit.

"[A] recent survey commissioned by Progressive Insurance found that 50 percent of 1,000 people surveyed said that they would change their driving habits as a result of increased costs at the pump."
—**Cincinnati Enquirer**

From the oceans sailed by Royal Caribbean to the skies traversed by Southwest, we have seen companies exhibit great skill and foresight in hedging oil price risks. In this next example, however, Progressive Insurance ratchets up this strategic chess game several notches as it astutely reenters an old market with a new pricing strategy.

Progressive Insurance Plays the Oil Price Card

"Don't play checkers in a chess world."
—**Ron Vara**

You first encountered Progressive Insurance in the chapter on human resources management. There, you saw Progressive executing a successful "cherry-picking" strategy during an economic downturn.

In this example, Progressive's "chess players" use the occasion of higher oil prices to lower auto insurance rates in a strategy designed to seize market share. The reasoning behind this rate cut illustrates the kind of high-level sophistication that at least some management teams have attained when crafting well-timed strategies in response to macroeconomic shocks.

In this regard, Progressive's executive team continually seeks to forecast movements in oil prices. When oil prices jump, Progressive knows from past experience that people will drive less. More subtly, consumers will also delay buying new cars as their discretionary incomes suffer from the "oil tax."

Why is this important from a pricing-strategy perspective? Simply because when people drive less *and* when fewer new cars are on the road, there are not just fewer accidents and insurance claims. There are also cheaper repair costs with fewer new cars and lower per-claim costs at auto body shops. These factors, in turn, mean that if a company such as Progressive can cut its rates *before* its competitors, it can grab additional market share—while at the same time increasing its profits.

This is exactly what happened with the oil price spike that began in 1999 with oil production cuts by OPEC and continued into 2000 with the red-hot global expansion. Prior to these oil price hikes, Progressive had purposely priced itself out of what it considered to be the underpriced auto insurance market. As oil prices crept up, however, Progressive moved to lower rates and reentered the market in force.

As Progressive's new rates took effect, its new revenues surged to more than 24 percent while its profit margins surged above 7 percent—more than twice the 3 percent average margin observed in the industry.

■■■ When Mother Nature Goes on a Rampage

■ El Pollo Loco correctly foresees that drought in Australia and the threat of Mad Cow disease in Canada will drive up prices first for beef and then eventually chicken. It uses fixed contracts to beat the price hikes.

"[W]hen it starts raining in Brazil to end a drought, it may well be time to buy Starbucks stock as the price of coffee is sure to fall even as Starbuck profit margins will rise."

—If It's Raining in Brazil, Buy Starbucks:
The Investor's Guide

In one of the most abiding images of "chaos theory," a butterfly flaps its wings in China and helps cause a typhoon halfway around the world. Other such forms of Mother Nature-inspired chaos range from El Niño conditions in Brazil and Africa that can slam coffee and cocoa prices; tsunamis off the coasts of Indonesia and Thailand that can, in turn, lead to epidemics of cholera and typhoid and increased demand for medicines; and a severe earthquake in Taiwan that drives up semiconductor prices while killing thousands.

The fact is Mother Nature can be a very cruel mistress. In this encore appearance, El Pollo Loco provides just one small example of how a company successfully coped with just two of her many threats—drought and disease.

The Logical Crazy Chicken Wrestles with Mad Cow

"While the federal government moves to increase assistance to drought-stricken farmers, questions are being asked about the future of Australia's core breeding stock. Farmers just cannot afford to feed their animals, and they are being sold and slaughtered. That will have a far-reaching effect on the cattle and sheep markets, even after the rains eventually come."

—Australian Broadcasting Company

This example beautifully highlights the actions of an executive team that correctly read the tea leaves of several exogenous shocks and appropriately hedged the "raw materials" cost of the major item on its production menu: chicken.

In this regard, many companies use sophisticated mathematical forecasting models to forecast the prices of their raw materials—and then hedge accordingly. Sometimes, however, it is simply enough for an executive team to have a global macroeconomic perspective in conjunction with a healthy dose of logic.

These particular attributes helped the El Pollo Loco purchasing department team parse the possibly far-ranging effects of several exogenous shocks on its supply chain. Beginning in 2002, severe drought and fires in Australia threatened to reduce Australian beef exports. Soon thereafter, the U.S. secretary of agriculture restricted Canadian beef imports because of Mad Cow disease concerns. On top of this, the beef market was facing smaller herds because of smaller and more expensive winter hay supplies.

So what's this got to do with chicken prices? Well, as the economically savvy El Pollo Loco purchasing team understood, as beef prices rose, there would be a "substitution effect" in which at least some people would switch to eating more chicken. Thus, the "supply shock" in the beef market would lead to increased demand for chicken and upward pressure on prices.

Because of a keen understanding of these economic relationships, El Pollo Loco's executive team was able to lock in fixed contracts for chicken *before* the price run-up and was not affected by the subsequent price spike.

▪▪▪ Leveraging Demographic Shifts

▪ KB Home successfully identifies two demographic trends—a burgeoning immigrant population and a Sun Belt retirement boom—and positions itself in the fastest-growing segments of the housing markets.

> *"Baby Boomers want second homes, their children are buying their first homes, and new immigrants are seeking to put down roots."*
>
> **—Investor's Business Daily**

At least when it comes to the housing market, legions of retiring Baby Boomers and a flood of new immigrants are hardly strange bedfellows. Together, these demographic groups represent two of the most potent sources of new housing demand ever witnessed, particularly in the ever-inviting Sunbelt states such as California and Arizona. It is precisely these kinds of powerful demographic forces that any self-respecting Master Cyclist executive team will seek to first identify and then go after, and KB Home proves to be no exception to this rule.

KB Home Does Its Demographic Homework

> *"In Rancho Cucamonga, KB Home is developing Huntington at Etiwanda, a subdivision of 48 homes offering third-car garages, voluminous formal entryways, gourmet kitchens and fine finishes that are selling in the $600,000s. A few miles away KB Home is simultaneously developing ... 156 homes in sixplexes expected open for sale in February in the mid $200,000s."*
>
> **—The Press Enterprise, Riverside, California**

We previously introduced the Master Cyclists of KB Home within the context of its KBnxt program—a production-to-order system for preselling homes that dramatically reduced the company's business cycle risk. This strategy was adopted in the wake of the 1990-1991 recession that left the company with a mountain of unsold inventory. But this was not KB Home's only strategic response.

In the wake of that recession, the company's executive team refocused its marketing position to target first-time home buyers. In KB Home's analysis, a big portion of first-time buyers is represented by the burgeoning immigrant population. KB Home saw these immigrants as a firm foundation for maintaining housing demand in the event of an economic downturn.

In addition, as the Baby Boomers have begun to retire to the Sunbelt—or build second homes—KB Home has also adopted a dual-track strategy in which it not only builds its smaller entry-level "sixplexes" for its first-time buyers. It also is offering luxury homes at three times the price with those "voluminous formal entryways" and "gourmet kitchens" referred to in the preceding excerpt. In this way, KB Home is able to cater its product offerings to simultaneously capitilize on two important demographic trends.

Regulatory and Legislative Shocks

- Guidant's "political animals" successfully lobby the Congress for passage of legislation that expedites its device approval process and creates new markets for several products.

- Fair Isaac strategically leverages the Patriot Act by augmenting its credit-scoring software suite with a money-laundering-detection and Patriot Act-compliant software module.

"The makers of medical devices are pouring millions of dollars into a congressional lobbying campaign designed to get their products to market faster and limit the Food and Drug Administration's oversight of manufacturing facilities."

—**Newhouse News Service**

Most exogenous shocks are severely negative and, by definition, hit companies *unexpectedly*. However, in at least some instances a company can use its lobbying prowess to proactively create its own quite positive "regulatory shock." That is why it is interesting to observe Guidant's "political animals" skillfully manipulate the legislative process to carve out several new markets while streamlining the regulatory process. In a slightly different vein, that is why it is equally interesting to see Fair Isaac very quickly and strategically expand its existing product line in response to a major legislative change triggered by the events of 9/11.

Guidant Creates Its Own "Regulatory Shock"

"Shaping a public policy environment that supports investment in medical innovation and timely patient access is a key strategic issue at Guidant."

—**Ron Dollens, CEO, Guidant**

"Under pressure from Congress and the Bush administration, the FDA has instituted industry-friendly measures that critics say further compromise safety."

—*U.S. News & World Report*

With sales of almost $4 billion to roughly 100 countries, Guidant is a global manufacturer of cardiovascular therapeutic devices and related products. Its products range from pacemakers and defibrillators to drug-coated stents, which are used to open blocked arteries of the heart.

In the late 1990s, a group co-chaired by Guidant aggressively lobbied Congress to pass the U.S. Food and Drug Administration Modernization Act. The purpose of this legislation was to speed up the approval process for medical solutions, and its signing into law by President Bill Clinton in 1997 had a very direct impact on Guidant's bottom line.

The new streamlined process not only enabled Guidant to bring four new products to market in just four months. The legislation also paved the way for Guidant to procure additional, and essential, R&D funding from venture capitalists who saw the prospect of bigger and faster rewards from new discoveries in a more regulatory-friendly environment.

It's important to note, however, that Guidant's political process was not an unambiguous blessing for the company's share-holders. In a sober reminder as to why regulations are often "necessary evils," Guidant would subsequently run into problems with its fast-tracked medicated stents that would force embarrassing recalls, a fall in the company's stock price, heightened scrutiny over the FDA's "vigilance" in monitoring safety problems, and significant problems with its acquisition by Johnson and Johnson.

Fair Isaac Expands in a Post 9/11 World

> *"In today's world, all government agencies have a heightened responsibility to safeguard our nation's infrastructure and people. At the same time, citizen rights must be protected to ensure that civil liberties are not violated. Fair Isaac's applications can help your government organization find the right balance in security management and privacy protection."*
> **—Fair Isaac Web site**

In an earlier chapter, you saw how the credit-scoring maven Fair Isaac exhibited exemplary patience in the execution of its acquisition strategy. Now you will see an equally astute strategic expansion of its product mix and tactical shift in its marketing message in response to the passage of the "Patriot Act" in the wake of the 9/11 attacks.

The Patriot Act is designed both to detect actual terrorists as well as to reveal any money-laundering efforts on behalf of terrorist networks. Under its far-reaching dictates, entities ranging from banks, insurance companies, and stockbrokers to casinos, pawnshops, and travel agents must collect information on customers whenever they open accounts. More important, these entities must *verify* that these customers are who they say they are and *determine* whether their names appear on any terrorist watch lists.

The Patriot Act also specifically requires financial institutions to check a terrorist list provided every two weeks by the U.S. Treasury's Financial Crimes Enforcement Network. Last, but hardly least, the Treasury's Office of Foreign Assets Control provides a similar list for cross-checking that identifies "specially designated nationals," "blocked persons," and "blocked entities" that have been allegedly associated with terrorism.

All of these new, post-9/11 regulatory requirements immediately created a huge new market of companies and financial institutions seeking to cost-effectively deal with a potentially onerous regulatory burden. By doing so, the Patriot Act also gave Fair Isaac a golden opportunity to build a Patriot Act-compliant "wartime" solution that could be added to its suite of existing, peacetime software credit-scoring and fraud-screening modules.

Expanding its product line was not Fair Isaac's only tactical move in response to 9/11, however. Fair Isaac also now markets its "risk manager for government" software with a heavy antiterrorist message. As the company's Web site touts, this system has applications in port and airport security, identification authorization, bioterrorism, and even military tactics.

As a final Master Cyclist benefit, by targeting the government sector more heavily in the wake of 9/11, Fair Isaac's executive team has found a less-cyclical—and highly lucrative!—revenue stream that contributes to a more stable earnings flow. In large part because of these new products, Fair Isaac increased its revenues by more than 60 percent in 2003—just two years after 9/11.

Key Points

- **The Dangers and Opportunities of Random Shocks**
  - Macroeconomic shocks range from war, terrorism, and oil price spikes to drought and disease.
  - Although macroeconomic shocks are, by definition, random, their after-effects are often quite logical and therefore possible to exploit with well-timed strategies and tactics.
  - Master Cyclist executive teams can quickly hedge prices, switch markets, strategically expand the product line, change the marketing message, or hedge particular risks in response to random shocks.
- **War, Terrorism, and When Mother Nature Rages**
  - War and terrorism give rise to the need for new products—from bomb-detection equipment to ceramic armor.
  - A drought in Australia can reduce beef exports and thereby raise U.S. chicken prices. Rain in Brazil leads to lower coffee bean prices and higher profit margins for coffee retailers. Business executives must regularly engage in this kind of "big-picture" thinking when parsing Mother Nature's economic implications.
- **Riding Demographic Waves and Exploiting Regulatory Shocks**
  - Demographic shifts represent some of the most powerful forces that shape the business environment. The Master Cyclist knows how to skillfully ride these demographic waves.
  - Most exogenous shocks are negative. However, in some cases, a company or industry can use its lobbying prowess to proactively create a positive "regulatory shock" that opens new markets, streamlines the regulatory process, or results in lower costs.

The Master Cyclist's Favorite Forecasting Tools

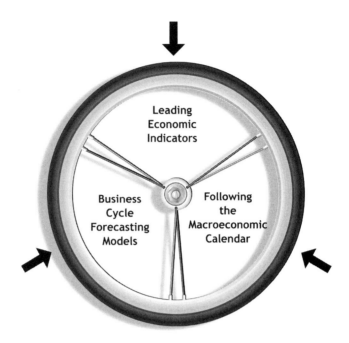

"Forecasting is always difficult, especially when it is about the future."

—The Economist

"There's no Holy Grail of economic forecasting; no magic indicator that's infallible."

—Lakshman Achuthan, Managing Director, Economic Cycle Research Institute

Managing the business cycle for competitive advantage means, first and foremost, learning how to forecast the business cycle in an accurate and timely manner. In this all-important task, the Master Cyclist relies on three sets of tools.

The first set consists of a select group of *leading economic indicators*. These include the "yield curve," stock and oil prices, the aptly named Index of Leading Indicators, and the even more useful "ECRI dashboard" of growth and inflation indicators.

The second set includes a variety of more complex *forecasting models*. As a final tool, there is the daily following of the monthly *macroeconomic calendar* of economic reports. Such reports are issued by government agencies and private institutions around the world on topics ranging from consumption, production, and trade to growth, inflation, and productivity. By studiously following this macroeconomic calendar, the Master Cyclist executive team can keep its finger most directly on the pulse of the business cycle—and thereby help improve the team's use of the other economic indicators and forecasting models it might rely on.

■■■ So Which "Leading Economic Indicators" Really Lead?

- The (almost) infallible yield curve stands tall atop the pyramid of Master Cyclist leading indicators.
- The stock market plays Sundance Kid to the yield curve's Butch Cassidy and emerges as a valuable co-leading indicator.
- Although both prove useful, the ECRI's "economic dashboard" decidedly trumps the Index of Leading Indicators on both accuracy and timeliness.
- Like a bad moon rising, higher oil prices almost always mean recessionary troubles are on the way.

*"**Leading indicator**: An economic indicator that changes before the economy has changed. ... There are also coincident indicators, which change about the same time as the overall economy, and lagging indicators, which change after the overall economy, but these are of minimal use as predictive tools."*

—**Investors.com**

The Master Cyclist knows that no single "leading economic indicator" is a perfect predictor of business cycle turning points. Even the best indicators occasionally flash false recessionary or expansionary signals. Therefore, the Master Cyclist closely follows a number of such indicators, each of which has been proven, in the crucible of repeated historical experience, to be very useful— if not infallible.

The Yield Curve Ain't No Ouija Board

> *"The yield curve inverted a full 12 months before the 2001 recession and more than half of corporate America blew off this highly reliable recessionary signal. How dumb is that?"*
>
> **—Ron Vara**

The yield curve measures the spread between short- and long-term interest rates on Treasury securities. It has proven to be a remarkably accurate signal of both recessionary and expansionary turning points and ranks at the top of the Master Cyclist's pyramid of leading indicators. Figure 11-1 shows the "four faces" of this (almost) infallible leading indicator at different points in time.

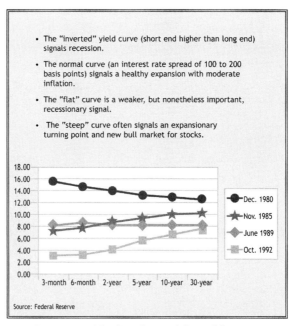

▲ **FIGURE 11-1** *The four faces of the yield curve.*

A "normal" yield curve such as the one observed in November 1985 indicates a healthy economic expansion without fear of inflation. The "spread" between short- and long-run rates is typically 100 to 200 basis points because long-term bond investors must receive a slightly higher return to compensate for time risk.

An "inverted" yield curve such as the one observed in December 1980 occurs when long-run interest rates fall *below* the short end of the curve. Such inversions have reliably signaled five out of the last six recessions over an eight-quarter horizon with only one false signal.

As for the "flat" yield curve observed in June 1989, every inverted curve must go through a flat phase. However, not every flat curve inverts. Still, a flat curve is an only slightly weaker signal of recession. Although it predicted all of the past six recessions within an eight-quarter horizon, it also had two false signals.

Finally, a "steep" yield curve occurs when the long end of the curve rises by more than the usual 100 to 200 basis point spread above the short end in anticipation of a coming robust expansion and possible inflationary pressures. This is exactly what happened in October 1992 to signal the beginning of what would become the longest economic boom in U.S. history. The prediction of this boom was no fluke. Steep curves have predicted fully five of the last six expansionary turning points.

Given the yield curve's excellent forecasting track record, it seems truly remarkable that so many corporate executives chose to ignore its strong recessionary warning signals leading up to the 2001 downturn. To see why the claims of CEOs such as John Chambers that "the brightest people in the world didn't see [the recession] coming" are so hollow, just consider Figure 11-2. It charts the ominous progression of the yield curve from its "normal" shape in June 1999 to the flat curve of November 1999 and finally to the recession-signaling inversion in March 2000.

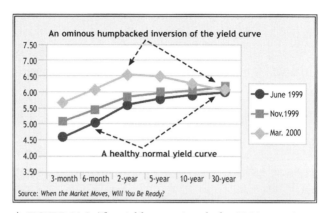

▲ **FIGURE 11-2** *The yield curve signals the 2001 recession.*

Note that the "humpbacked" March 2000 yield curve clearly inverts between the 2-year and 10-year securities. *This is exactly one year before the 2001 recession would officially begin.* It is also the very month that the stock market cataclysmically started its long, extended collapse.

As to why the yield curve behaves in this fashion—and why it is such a powerful forecasting signal—*it is well worth just a brief digression here to discuss the underlying logic of the yield curve's movements.*

The Abiding Logic of the Yield Curve

> *"The Federal Reserve's decision this week to raise interest rates in order to ward off inflation was, as expected, criticized from all corners. Manufacturers warned that higher interest rates would drive up costs and drive away consumers. Labor unions predicted layoffs. Politicians feared disgruntled voters."*
> *[emphasis added]*
>
> *—New York Times*

Understanding the logic of the yield curve's forecasting power begins with the observation that *short-run* versus *long-run* interest rates are determined by two completely different entities. Note, however, that this subtle distinction is not evident in the preceding excerpt from the *New York Times*, which refers simply to "interest rates." This is very typical—but very imprecise!—journalism, even from excellent newspapers like the *Times*.

In fact, only short-run interest rates are *directly* determined by the U.S. Federal Reserve. When the Fed is concerned about rising inflationary pressures, it begins raising two short-term rates—the "federal funds rate," which is the rate on overnight loans between banks, and the "discount rate," which is the rate the Fed charges banks to borrow short-term funds.[1]

Note, however, that *it would be very wrong to assume that just because the Fed raises short-run rates that long-term interest rates necessarily must also rise.* In fact, whether long-term interest rates rise—or fall!—in response to Fed rate hikes depends *indirectly* on how long-term bond investors react to the Fed's contractionary policies. To understand why, consider this typical yield curve inversion scenario.

After a sustained economic expansion, inflationary pressures begin to build. This provokes the Fed to embark on a new cycle of contractionary rate hikes to quell these inflationary pressures.

Of course, the Fed's goal is to bring the economy in for a "soft landing." That is, the Fed wants to slow the economy down enough to reduce inflationary pressures—but not enough to trigger a recession.

Now here's the problem: After repeated short-run rate hikes by the Fed, long-bond investors might begin to believe that an overaggressive Fed is raising interest rates too high and too fast. At this point, these bond investors become far less concerned about inflation and far more concerned that the Fed's highly contractionary monetary policy will trigger a recession.

At this critical turning point, long-bond investors begin to expect recession and deflation rather than expansion and inflation. Because long-run interest rates always fall in a deflationary environment, bond investors therefore begin to more heavily buy long-term bonds. This they do to "lock in" the current, more attractive long-term rate.

Here is what is interesting: This speculative buying activity, in turn, drives bond prices up, and yields on the long end of the curve correspondingly fall—even as the Fed continues to hike short-run rates. Initially, this causes the yield curve to flatten as the short end rises and the long end falls. Eventually, the curve might invert—as Figure 11-2 shows it did as a prelude to the 2001 recession.

The broader forecasting point we can extract from this very typical scenario is this: *The yield curve is such a powerful forecasting tool precisely because it embodies the collective wisdom of millions of highly sophisticated investors quite literally putting trillions of dollars on the table in highly intelligent speculative bets on the direction of the business cycle.* That is about as far from Ouija board forecasting as you can get!

Accordingly, every aspiring Master Cyclist executive team interested in effectively managing the business cycle should keep its collective thumb on the pulse of the yield curve and its movements. This is extremely easy to do. Business executives can find a daily snapshot of the yield curve on any one of a number of Web sites such as www.bloomberg.com or www.smartmoney. com.[2]

The Stock Market's Early Bear Crystal Ball

"The stock market has predicted nine out of the last five recessions"
—Nobel Laureate Paul Samuelson

"[S]tock prices provide information that is not contained in the yield curve so that a combination of these two indicators performed better than the yield curve alone."
—Professors Arturo Estrella and Frederic Mishkin[3]

As with the yield curve, the stock market's forecasting power comes from its expression of the collective wisdom of investors on the future direction of the economy. In this case, however, it is equity rather than bond investors doing the "forecasting."

So how exactly does this work? Well, the predictive power of the stock market anchors on the assumption that stock prices reflect investor expectations about a future stream of earnings. Because a recession means lower earnings for most companies, stock prices must fall as expectations of a recession rise. Of course, just the opposite must be true regarding expectations of an expansion.

In addition to this direct link between stock prices and business cycle movements, a more indirect link relates to a so-called "wealth effect." When the stock market goes up, investors are willing to consume more. This willingness can have a highly stimulative and expansionary effect on the business cycle.

Of course, when the stock market collapses—as it began to do in March 2000—the wealth effect goes into reverse. Consumers pull in their shopping horns, and the business cycle becomes more vulnerable to a downturn.

Although these are very good reasons why stock price movements should presage movements in the business cycle, the stock market's "crystal ball" has taken a lot of heat for its sometimes false recessionary signals. Just consider Professor Samuelson's oft-cited quip in the preceding excerpt about how the stock market has predicted nine of the last five recessions. It is important to point out, however, that this famous quip came off the Nobel Laureate's cuff way back in 1965. That was then. This is now.

In truth, the "now" of the stock market's real predictive power is much more accurately captured in the competing excerpt from Professors Arturo Estrella and Frederic Mishkin. Their comprehensive statistical work in the 1990s has demonstrated that following stock prices alone can be deceiving at times. However, when the information contained in stock prices is added to the information embedded in the yield curve, the predictive power of both go up! That is why both the yield curve and stock prices play prominent roles in the composition of our next two forecasting tools—the aptly named Index of Leading Indicators and the even more powerful ECRI dashboard.

The Index of Leading Economic Indicators— Warts and All

Several different rules of thumb have been applied to the [Index of Leading Indicators] to determine whether it is signaling a recession. ... [T]he most common rule is that three successive declines in the index forecast a recession within the next nine months.

By this rule the traditional index has successfully predicted eight of the nine U.S. recessions since 1948, with leads of two to eight months. But it has also given seven false signals.

—**Theodore Crone and Kevin Babyak, analysts, Federal Reserve Bank of Philadelphia**

The Conference Board's Index of Leading Economic Indicators (LEI) consists of 10 components, and it might not surprise you after the earlier discussion to learn that the yield curve and stock prices account for fully *one third* of the index's weighting.

The LEI also includes the "real money supply" to gauge the easiness or tightness of credit, an index of consumer expectations to plumb the strength of future demand, and average weekly manufacturing hours and manufacturers' new orders to gauge the strength of the supply side of the economy. In addition, average weekly hours in manufacturing and average weekly initial claims for unemployment insurance are included to get a read on the job market, while building permits serve as a proxy for housing market activity.

Finally, the arguably most obscure component of the LEI is "vendor performance." It measures how long it takes for companies to deliver their goods. The contrarian idea is that delays and bottlenecks in the delivery system signal a more robust economy, whereas quick deliveries signal a slowdown.

As for the forecasting performance of the LEI, we can see from the preceding excerpt from Theodore Crone and Kevin Babyak— two analysts at the Federal Reserve Bank of Philadelphia—that the track record has been less than stellar. The problem is not that the LEI has not reliably predicted recessions. Instead, it just gives far too many "false signals." Moreover, it performs poorly in signaling expansionary turning points.

For these (and several other) reasons, I much prefer the next set of leading indicators—those that appear on the ECRI dashboard.

Navigating the Business Cycle Using the ECRI Dashboard

"Think of two indexes as the temperature and fuel gauges on your economic dashboard. You don't need to be a car mechanic to be able to read the fuel level and the engine temperature of your car. Similarly, monthly glances at the [Future Inflation Gauge] will allow you to assess how hot the economy is running. The Weekly Leading Index will tell you if the economy is ready to race forward or about to run out of gas."

—Lakshman Achuthan and Anirvan Banerji, ECRI

The Economic Cycle Research Institute (ECRI) was founded more than 50 years ago by Geoffrey Moore—an economist and statistician who is often rightly described as the "father of leading indicators." It was Moore who, in 1950, came up with the first list of leading economic indicators. It was Moore who, eight years later, developed the composite index method. And it was Moore who, in 1967, debuted the original Index of Leading Indicators just discussed.

Today, ECRI remains on the cutting edge of economic forecasting. In fact, it has developed a customized "economic dashboard" that many Fortune 500 companies regularly use to track the economy.

The first gauge on this dashboard is the Weekly Leading Index. It uses a more compact set of seven leading indicators than the LEI and has been designed to turn down before a recession and turn up before a recovery. Like the LEI, it prominently features both the yield curve and stock prices. In addition, it includes corporate bond spreads, mortgage applications, jobless claims, the money supply, and a price index. One of the big advantages of the ECRI Weekly Leading Index over the LEI is that it is weekly—and therefore much more timely.

The second dashboard component is called the Future Inflation Gauge, or FIG. It represents an index composed of eight indicators that measure price and wage inflation and movements in interest rates.

Together, these two gauges on the ECRI dashboard provide business executives a very simple but powerful forecasting tool. That this is so should be evident in this extended excerpt about a division of DuPont from the excellent book *Beating the Business Cycle* by two key members of the ECRI brain trust, managing director Lakshman Achuthan and research director Anirvan Banerji:

DuPont has been a client of ECRI's for many years. ... In the fall of 1998, in the wake of the Russian default and the LTCM debacle, President Clinton warned the country of what he thought was the worst financial crisis in 50 years. The Fed, in response, made three emergency rate cuts. Recession fears became widespread. But while apprehensive competitors were cutting prices, [DuPont] held its ground because the ECRI leading indexes it monitored did not show a downturn ahead. As a result, it was able to handily outperform its competitors.

In late 1999, with the boom back on track, complacency had once again set in. However, the leading indexes that related to their business were pointing to a cyclical downturn in late 2000. Knowing that, [DuPont] took preemptive steps, aggressively pushing sales and reducing inventories in the first half, in anticipation of a lean second half. When industry demand began to slump in the second half of 2000, they were well positioned, having already pared down inventories.

As a final word on the accuracy and timeliness of the ECRI dashboard, there are these words of flattery from the *Economist*, a publication not known for its lavish praise: "ECRI was one of the few firms to forecast both of the past two recessions. Its leading indicators for other economies have also fared well. It successfully forecast recessions in Japan in 1997 and 2001."

The broader point: Navigate your company with the help of the ECRI dashboard and you will have a much better chance of avoiding recessionary potholes.

A Bad Recessionary Moon Rising with Oil Prices

> *"Eight of the nine post-World War II recessions were accompanied by sharp increases in the price of oil. The last four recessions followed this pattern: the 1973–1975 recession followed the oil embargo; the double dip recession of 1980–1982 followed the second oil shock, which was caused by the Iranian revolution and Iran-Iraq war; the 1990–1991 recession followed the oil price spike induced by the Gulf war; and the 2001 recession followed a sharp rise in oil prices from 1999-2000. This would seem to be persuasive evidence that oil prices play a strong role in determining the business cycle."*
> **—Marc Labonte, Congressional Research Service**

For U.S. corporations, the oil price shock indicator is particularly important. Currently, the United States is home to less than 5 percent of the world's population but accounts for more than 25 percent of world oil consumption. Because it only produces a little more than 10 percent of the world's oil supply, the United States must import more than half of its 20-million-barrel-per-day habit. Adding to the strategic and political risks of this heavy oil import dependence, more than half of U.S. imports flow from the monopolistic OPEC cartel.

As to why rising oil prices have historically played such an important role in triggering recessions, there is this obvious *supply-side* effect: Higher oil prices drive up production costs. Forced to raise prices, producers then sell fewer goods. They, in turn, begin to produce less—and lay off people accordingly.

On the *demand* side, every time OPEC cuts production and raises prices, this acts as a "tax" on domestic consumers and lowers their purchasing power. To put it most simply, if it costs more to fill up the gas tank, less money is left over for a trip to the mall or a movie or the dry cleaner. Moreover, because the "tax revenues" go to foreigners, there is no government to reinvest the tax proceeds into the domestic economy.

Note, however, that although oil price shocks have been associated with every recession since 1973, not every oil price shock will always lead to recession—as we saw in 2003 when the global economy boomed despite such a run-up. This is why, just as with a jury in a court of law, it is important for the Master Cyclist to follow *all* the important economic indicators and always look at the direction in which the "preponderance of evidence" points. That way, the Master Cyclist is less likely to be fooled by any false signal of a single indicator.

■■■ The Blue Chip of Forecasting Models

■ The Blue Chip Consensus Survey turns the forecasting gang that couldn't shoot straight into a sharper marksman.

"Forecasts produced by economic models with hundreds of equations are notoriously bad at predicting recessions because they tend to extrapolate the recent past. This leads to big forecasting errors near turning points, because recessions are caused by abrupt changes in the behavior of firms and consumers."

—The Economist

"Economic forecasts deserve to be taken seriously, not necessarily because they promise to be accurate but because they are more useful than having no forecasts at all."

—Peter Bernstein and Theodore Silbert,
Harvard Business Review

Some forecasting models are built using traditional Keynesian economic assumptions. Other models reflect monetarist or supply-side economic assumptions. Still others are rooted in the theory of "rational expectations" or represent some synthesis of *all* the competing schools of macroeconomic thought. Nonetheless, what all forecasting models share in common is the singular and unsettling fact that they are sometimes very wrong—as the preceding excerpt from the *Economist* suggests. Just consider this startlingly fact: Most forecasters missed the 2001 recession!

This observation leads us to the most important point of this very brief discussion of economic forecasting models: *One of the more efficient ways for any executive team to process the available forecasting data is to subscribe to the Blue Chip Consensus Survey.*

The Blue Chip survey has been published for more than 25 years and includes forecasts of 15 macroeconomic variables, including most importantly GDP, the Consumer Price Index, the unemployment rate, and the 3-month and 10-year Treasury securities.

Survey participants number roughly 50 and range from major investment banks such as Chase Manhattan and corporations such as Motorola to consulting firms such as Global Insight and academic institutions such as UCLA.

Note, however, that in an important study, Andy Bauer, Robert Eisenbeis, Daniel Waggoner, and Tao Zha found that any single forecast is likely to be prone to considerable error, whereas *the Blue Chip Consensus forecast "performs better than any individual forecaster."*[4]

This observation again reinforces the point that *a true Master Cyclist relies on many sources of information to form expectations about the direction of the business cycle—and plans accordingly.* This observation also helps make the case that it is well worth following the broader "macroeconomic calendar," which we now discuss to complete this chapter.

■■■ The Macroeconomic Calendar's Daily Dance of Data

■ *Sans* any provocative pinups, the macroeconomic calendar still delivers an exciting forecasting experience for the discerning Master Cyclist.

"The [macroeconomic] calendar provides the daily dance of data that is the single most important source of fuel that moves the stock market."
—***When the Market Moves, Will You Be Ready?***

That the "daily dance of data" does indeed move the financial markets should be evident in these examples:

1. The Consumer Price Index comes out unexpectedly hot and raises fears that the Federal Reserve will more aggressively hike interest rates. In reaction, the prices of stocks plummet in sectors sensitive to the interest rate such as autos, housing, and financial services.

2. The monthly trade deficit balloons, and the dollar plunges. However, the stock prices of companies in export industries such as agriculture, aircraft, and business services get a nice bullish bump up on the assumption that with a cheaper dollar, they will sell more goods to foreigners.

3. News from the Department of Commerce that it has upwardly revised the fourth quarter GDP growth rate hits the wire early in the morning before the stock market opens. With the economic recovery apparently alive and well, the S&P futures zoom into the green.

This "daily dance of data" is equally important to business executives, albeit over a longer time horizon. *By diligently following the macroeconomic calendar, the Master Cyclist executive team can effectively become its own economic forecaster.* Moreover, by watching on a regular basis how the stock, bond, and currency markets react to each new piece of economic news, any would-be Master Cyclist can go a long way toward building both financial market literacy and a savvy business cycle "sixth sense" about where the economy might be heading.

Table 11-1 provides a list of some of the most important economic reports released every month in the United States.[5] However, I hasten to add here that it can be equally important to be aware of economic reportage from other countries, too.

For example, a report from Japan or Germany indicating a falling GDP or rising unemployment can have a big negative impact on a U.S. exporting company. Similarly, a rapidly growing Indian or Chinese GDP can push up the prices of oil and steel in the United States—and contribute to a recession-triggering oil price shock. So always remember to "think globally"—no matter how local your business.

▲ **TABLE 11-1**   *The U.S. Monthly Macroeconomic Calendar*

1. Construction Spending	Department of Commerce	First business day of the month
2. Purchasing Managers' Index	National Association of Purchasing Managers	First business day of the month
3. Personal Income & Consumption	Department of Commerce	First business day of the month
4. Auto and Truck Sales	Department of Commerce	Third business day of the month
5. The Jobs Report	Department of Labor	First Friday of the month
6. Index of Leading Indicators	Conference Board	First week of the month
7. Consumer Credit	Federal Reserve	Fifth business day of the month
8. Productivity & Costs*	Department of Labor	Around the seventh of the second month of quarter for prior quarter
9. Retail Sales	Department of Commerce	Between the eleventh and fourteenth of the month
10. Producer Price Index	Department of Labor	Around the eleventh of each month for the prior month
11. Industrial Production & Capacity Utilization	Federal Reserve	Around the fifteenth of the month
12. Business Inventories	Department of Commerce	Around the fifteenth of the month
13. Consumer Price Index	Department of Labor	Between the fifteenth and twenty-first of the month
14. Housing Starts	Department of Commerce	Between the sixteenth and twentieth of the month
15. International Trade	Department of Commerce	Around the twentieth of the month
16. Consumer Confidence	Conference Board University of Michigan Survey Research Center	Last Tuesday of the month; second and last weekend of the month
17. The Federal Budget	U.S. Treasury	Third week of the month
18. Durable Goods Orders	Department of Commerce	Third or fourth week of the month

19. Factory Orders	Department of Commerce	About a week after the Durable Goods report
20. Employment Cost Index	Department of Labor	Near the end of the month for the quarter for the prior quarter
21. Existing Home Sales	National Association of Realtors	Around the twenty-fifth of the month
22. New Home Sales	Department of Commerce	Around the last business day of the month
23. GDP	Department of Commerce	Quarterly; third or fourth week of the month

*Quarterly reports in *italic*; all others are monthly.

The Strategic Power of the Patterns of Sector Rotation

- Citigroup brilliantly "flips" Travelers Insurance for billions in a stellar example of profitably playing the "sector-rotation" game.

"Sector rotation in the market continues on Wall Street as investors do an about-face out of blue chip stocks into tech issues."

—CNN

"If you are in the right sector at the right time, you can make a lot of money very fast."

—Peter Lynch

It is perhaps fitting to end this chapter about learning how to anticipate and forecast movements in the business cycle with a more in-depth discussion of the critical concept of *sector rotation* (a concept introduced in Chapter 3, The Acquisitive Master Cyclist Buys Low and Sells High"). The broader goal here is one of great strategic and tactical importance: to cultivate a more sophisticated awareness of the many industry and sector cycles that move in and out of phase with the broader business and stock market cycles.

Distilled to its essence, sector rotation refers to this readily observable phenomenon: Although most stock prices rise in a bull market and fall in a bear market, over different phases of the "stock market cycle," certain industry sectors tend to "outperform" others. Figure 11-3 charts these typical patterns of sector rotation in the stock market as they move in and out of phase with the companion business cycle.

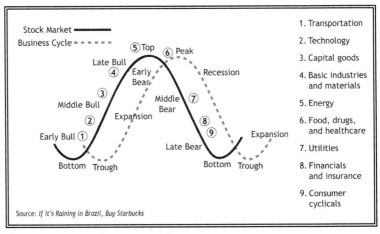

▲ **FIGURE 11-3** *The patterns of sector rotation.*

Note first in the figure that, as already discussed in this chapter, the stock market tends to be a "leading indicator" of the business cycle. That is, the stock market moves bullishly upward in anticipation of economic recovery and reaches its "top" well before the business cycle peaks and heads down into recession. This is why, again as noted earlier, the Master Cyclist pays very close attention to the stock market when seeking to anticipate and forecast movements in the business cycle.

As important, however, the Master Cyclist also pays very close attention to the demonstrable patterns of sector rotation depicted in the figure. You can see, for example, that the stock prices of "consumer cyclicals" such as autos and housing (the 9th sector in the chart) along with sectors such as transportation (1) and technology (2) typically tend to outperform other sectors in the Late Bear and Early Bull phases of the stock market cycle. Just why is this so?

Well, by the Late Bear phase, the Federal Reserve has significantly cut interest rates in the hopes of stimulating the economy. At this point, there is pent-up demand for big-ticket items such as cars and houses as people have hoarded their cash while riding out the recession; and with the glimmer of a recovery on the horizon, this pent-up demand is unleashed. As consumers begin to splurge on these big-ticket items, other sectors such as transportation (1) and technology (2) come roaring back to life. Anticipating an attendant spurt in profits in these sectors, investors buy their stocks and drive stock prices sharply up.

In contrast, other so-called defensive sectors such as food and pharmaceuticals (6) will each have their day the Early Bear sun. This is because, as the prospect of a recession looms, investors will be more attracted to the relative safety of the far more stable earnings of these "noncyclicals," which people continue to demand even in recessions. After all, people have to eat, and sick people need drugs no matter what the economic conditions.

Finally, note that the energy sector (5) tends to peak in the Late Bull phase of the stock market. At this point, the economy is humming along at full capacity and at a feverish pitch. In this "boom" time, a combination of heavy energy demand and constrained energy supplies can lead to a very sharp run-up in energy prices. Anticipating this run-up and the sharp boost in energy company earnings that it portends, investors pile into energy stocks and drive up their prices.

As you have learned in this chapter, the unfortunate result of any sharp run-up in energy prices is often a collateral slowing of the economy. That is why oil price shocks tend to be a very useful leading economic indicator of recession.

The next example illustrates just one of the many strategic and tactical applications of this concept of sector rotation in Master Cyclist management. What is perhaps most interesting about this example of a very well-timed acquisition *and* divestiture by

Citigroup is that the sector that we focus on—insurance (eight)—is one in which stock prices tend to move *countercyclically* with the business cycle. This is because insurance is likewise a defensive sector, which stock investors prefer in recessionary times because of the stability of its earnings.

Citigroup "Flips" Over Travelers

> *"Sandy Weill got control of Citibank in 1998 by merging his insurance company Travelers Group into it. The combination ... put Weill in charge of the world's largest financial-services empire. Now, like a man kicking away a ladder after he has ascended it, Weill proposes to spin off the property and casualty division of Travelers."*

> **—Michael Sivy, CNN/Money**

Citigroup's stellar sector-rotation play rightfully begins in early 1998 when the legendary Sandy Weill was still CEO of the insurance conglomerate Travelers. At this time, Weill approached Citicorp's CEO, John Reed, and pitched what would come to be known as the "mother of all mergers"—one that created a corporate powerhouse with more than 100 million customers in more than 100 countries generating more than $50 billion in revenue and sitting on more than $1 trillion in assets.

In fact, this merger was so big that it actually broke the law—specifically, the provisions of the so-called Glass-Steagall Act. This federal law had been passed during the Great Depression to prevent commercial banks from getting into the insurance business.

It is an interesting tale of American power politics as to how Weill and Reid successfully lobbied the Federal Reserve and Congress to remove the Glass-Steagle strictures and allow the merger.[6] It is an equally interesting tale of Machiavellian in-fighting and intrigue as to how it turned out that the hard-driving "Emperor" Sandy Weill and not the cerebral John Reed eventually wound up as CEO at the helm of the newly formed Citigroup. However, from a Master Cyclist point of view, what is really most interesting is the multi-billion-dollar sector-rotation "chess move" that Weill would make "flipping" Travelers' stock just a few years after gaining control of Citigroup. Figure 11-4 illustrates this brilliant sector-rotation play.

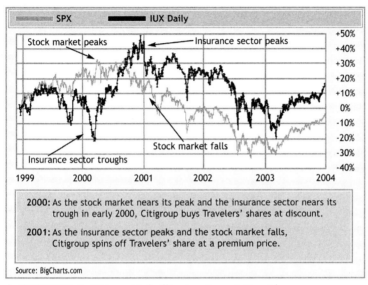

▲ FIGURE 11-4 *Citigroup's brilliant sector-rotation play.*

Note first how the stock market, as indicated by the movement of the S&P 500 index, peaks in early 2000. This happens *even as the underperforming insurance sector index IUX is reaching a trough.*

It is at this propitious point that Weill's Citigroup makes a cash offer to purchase all the shares outstanding of Travelers Property Casualty Corp. The result of the tender offer is that Citigroup winds up in April 2000 picking up more than 52 million shares at a bargain price.

Now look again carefully at the figure. You can also see the insurance sector surging to a new high in late 2000 and early 2001 *even as the stock market is falling precipitously.* In fact, this is a textbook case of sector rotation as investors flee out of volatile tech and energy stocks and run for the safety of the now-outperforming insurance sector.

At this equally propitious point, Weill executed what has been described at the "perfect spinoff" of Travelers. It became the sixth largest IPO in history and the largest insurance offering.

This tactical sector-rotation play not only netted Citigroup several billion dollars. It also allowed Citigroup to strategically and profitably exit from an insurance business that was the slowest growing part of the company—a business that the Citibank side of Citicorp had never really warmed to.

▪ Key Points

- ▪ **The Master Cyclist Forecasting Toolbox**
  - The Master Cyclist uses a select set of "leading economic indicators" and forecasting models and follows the macroeconomic calendar to forecast business cycle turning points in an accurate and timely manner.
- ▪ **An Overview of the "Leading Economic Indicators"**
  - The yield curve is a very powerful forecasting tool because it embodies the collective wisdom of bond market investors speculating on the future direction of the economy.
  - Yield curve inversions signal recessions. Steep curves signal expansions.
  - The stock market's predictive power derives largely from the fact that stock prices reflect investor expectations about a future stream of earnings. Stock prices must fall as expectations of a recession and lower earnings rise, and vice versa.
  - The ECRI economic dashboard has two gauges: a Weekly Leading Index and a Future Inflation Gauge. This dashboard has proven to be a more powerful and timely tool than the Index of Leading Indicators and many forecasting models.

- Eight of the nine post-World War II recessions have been accompanied by sharp increases in the price of oil, including the past four recessions.

A Very Short Forecasting Model Story

- One of the most efficient ways for an executive team to process the available forecasting data is to subscribe to the Blue Chip Consensus Survey, which has performed better than any individual forecaster.

The Wisdom of Following the Macro-economic Calendar

- By diligently following the macroeconomic calendar, the Master Cyclist team can effectively become its own forecaster.

- By watching how the stock, bond, and currency markets react to each new piece of economic news, executives can build both financial market literacy and a savvy business cycle "sixth sense" about where the economy might be heading.

Tuning in to the Patterns of Sector Rotation

- Although most stock prices rise in a bull market and fall in a bear market, over different phases of the "stock market cycle," certain industry sectors tend to "outperform" others.

- Cultivating an awareness of these patterns of sector rotation has great strategic and tactical value for the Master Cyclist.

Concluding Thoughts

"Anyone can steer the ship when the sea is calm."

—Publius Syrus

po·lyph·o·ny *(n): A style of musical composition in which two or more independent melodies are juxtaposed in harmony.*

There is a "sweet spot" in the expansionary phase of the business cycle where virtually all activities of the corporation move—and *should* move—in the same direction. Managing a company during this sweet spot is as easy as steering a ship in calm seas.

Of course, the true measure of the corporate executive team comes not in these bullish times. Nor does it come during a symmetrically bearish "dead spot"—that dark recessionary interval of the business cycle when virtually all functions have been put in reverse and corporate executives wait behind a veil of uncertainty for the first glimmer of recovery.

Rather, the true measure of a corporation's executive team comes in its ability—or lack thereof—to manage "polyphonically" at critical points and turning points in the business cycle. At such points, the polyphonic corporation begins to harmonically blend both pro- and countercyclical strategies and tactics into an ever-changing and highly profitable mix as it presciently seeks to gain advantage over its rivals and position itself for the next sweet spot or dead zone.

The purpose of this book has been to illustrate this Master Cyclist polyphony of well-timed strategies and tactics over the course of the business cycle. In this task, I have tried to present the material in an as accessible and entertaining way as possible.

My abiding hope is that the key points and insights of this book sufficiently motivate any executive team—regardless of company size—to embrace the lessons of Master Cyclist management as a means of creating value for their firm and crafting a sharp and leading competitive edge over rivals.

Now that you have heard from me, I would very much like to hear from you. This is particularly true if you are an executive or manager or employee with your own story to tell about how your company managed the business cycle well—or poorly.

You can easily reach me by e-mail through my Web site at *www.peternavarro.com*. I also urge any reader wanting to stay abreast of the latest developments in Master Cyclist management to frequently check this Web site; my research team continues to add compelling examples to an already extensive list.

To end, I want to leave you with these words of hockey great Wayne Gretzky, whose style of play on the ice perfectly captures both the essence and spirit of Master Cyclist management. Gretzky says this about his scoring strategy:

> *I don't skate to where the puck is. I skate to where the puck is going to be.*

> **—Peter Navarro**
> **www.peternavarro.com**

The Master Cyclist Project's Treasure Trove of Data and All-Star Team

"Are we merely studying a set of companies that just happened by luck to stumble into the right set of decisions? Or was there something distinctive about their process that dramatically increased the likelihood of being right?"

—**Jim Collins,** *Good to Great*

I began the Master Cyclist Project at the University of California-Irvine's Merage School of Business in September 2000 as an analytical, integrative, and experiential vehicle to teach MBA students in my core curriculum macroeconomics courses how to strategically manage business cycle risk. This project was built on the foundations of three of my own professional experiences.

■■ Corporate Strategy Tells Us Only "Why" but Not "When"

"Strategy answers two questions: Where do you want to go? And how do want to get there?"

—**Professor Kathleen Eisenhardt and Shona Brown**[1]

As a doctoral student at Harvard University in the 1980s, Professor Richard Caves introduced me to one of the most interesting and applied fields in all of economics: *industrial organization.* This field constitutes the intellectual backbone of modern corporate strategy as it is typically taught in MBA programs.

In fact, it was a much earlier student of Caves—corporate strategy guru Michael Porter—who, in essence, "crossed the Charles River" over to the Harvard Business School and repackaged the insights of industrial organization into the best-selling book *Competitive Strategy*—a textbook and gospel of many business school strategy courses.

*The problem, however, with corporate strategy as it is taught today in many top business schools is that it is essentially a static analysis. That is, corporate strategy discusses in great detail **how*** *static or time-independent factors such as economies of scale or the degree of product differentiation will determine industry structure and competitive advantage and **why** certain strategic decisions to acquire or expand or diversify should be made. However, the strategy literature is largely silent on the "**when**" or timing of implementing such strategic decisions. This is precisely where the equally critical **dynamic** role of movements in the business cycle and events and shocks in the broader macroeconomic environment come into strategic play.*

For example, as you have seen in this book, sound corporate strategy might dictate that a firm acquire a key rival to improve price margins or perhaps vertically integrate to cut costs by acquiring a key supplier. However, the timing of such acquisitions critically depends on which particular phase that the business cycle—and the related stock market and interest rate cycles—might be in. This is because the acquiring firm might want to wait for the appropriate time in these cycles when stock prices or interest rates are likely to be falling to make sure the strategic acquisitions are truly accretive to earnings.

Perhaps not surprisingly, this lack of any systematic theory of the role of the business cycle in the timing of corporate strategy and tactics is reflected in a similar oversight in the boardrooms of many corporations—and many MBA classrooms! Indeed, far too many executives are, as I have referred to them in this book, Reactive Cyclists. That is, they react to, rather than skillfully ride, the business cycle and invariably wind up in this classic trap: They continue to ramp up production, employment, and even capital expansion late into the expansionary cycle—even as they borrow funds at premium rates and hire more workers at premium wages.

Inevitably, these Reactive Cyclists find themselves stuck with huge inventory overhangs, idle workers, and a big squeeze on their cash flow when the recession hits. It is precisely these gaps in both the corporate strategy literature and accepted best-management practices that the research and key findings of the Master Cyclist Project have sought to fill.

▪▪▪ If It's Raining in Brazil, Buy Starbucks!

My second professional experience underlying the Master Cyclist project has been my ongoing research into the relationship between movements in the business cycle and movements in the *stock market*. The most accessible statement of this research is contained in my book *If It's Raining in Brazil, Buy Starbucks*.[2] In that book for stock market investors, I illustrated how stock prices respond to complex changes in the business cycle and the broader global macroeconomic environment. In *Brazil*, I also illustrated how to profitably invest from a "big-picture" point of view.

What is relevant here about this macroeconomic approach to stock market investing is this: In the very broadest sense, *little differentiates what motivates investors to buy the stock of a particular company and what motivates executives within that company to make decisions about such things as production levels, pricing, marketing, staffing, the timing of capital expenditures, and so on.*

Indeed, both investors and executives place the same kind of speculative bets on which way the business cycle is likely to head and at what pace the economy will move to get there. Therefore, it has been a very easy reach for me to go from the *Brazil* book's business cycle-sensitive stock market investing framework to developing the Master Cyclist framework for managing the business cycle for competitive advantage.

▪▪▪ Teaching Our MBAs Well

My final professional experience upon which the Master Cyclist Project has been built involves my ongoing research into the field of management education. In this regard, it is very unusual for business school professors such as myself to actually systematically study the tenets of sound pedagogy. Instead, many of my colleagues learn to teach simply by "doing it"—and, in the "publish-or-perish" world of academia, spend most of their time on their research.

In my particular case, I came to the pedagogy literature first in the mid-1990s through a rigorously designed project on the UCI campus to teach economics in a "virtual classroom," cyber-learning format.[3] Several years later, I also had occasion to review a vast "reformist" management education literature as part of the background research for my 2005 book *What the Best MBAs Know*.

From these research journeys into what constitutes "best practices" in management education, I learned that any truly effective curriculum to train budding business executives in the art and science of management must necessarily be (1) strategic in its outlook, (2) global in its perspective, (3) integrative in its curriculum approach, and (4) experiential in its methods.[4]

The Master Cyclist Project was expressly designed to help achieve the first and second goals in my macroeconomics classes by filtering the compelling executive need to better understand the global macroeconomic environment directly through equally compelling considerations of management strategy.

The third goal of curriculum integration is achieved as students learn to apply macroeconomic analysis and the principles of Master Cyclist management across the spectrum of organizational activities—from production, inventory control, and supply chain management to marketing, capital expenditures, and various acquisition/divestiture, diversification, and hedging strategies.

As for the fourth experiential goal, it is achieved by requiring students to directly interact with the executives and managers of the organizations they are assigned to analyze from a Master Cyclist perspective. This they do through both formal interviews and informal discussions with key management team members.

■■ An Army of MBA Talent and Treasure Trove of Data and Examples

The serendipitous result of this Master Cyclist teaching process has been (1) the marshaling of a large army of highly skilled MBA analytical talent; (2) a resultant accumulation of a treasure trove of examples on both how—and how not—to properly manage the business cycle for competitive advantage; (3) the aggregation of the individual company research into a large database for more formal statistical analysis; and, ultimately, (4) the determination of the key concepts, findings, insights, and points of the project that have been presented in this book.

I have greatly enjoyed developing this project and urge anyone who wants more information about it to visit the Master Cyclist Project link at my Web site at www.peternavarro.com. Finally, I want to salute all the students who have worked on this project over the years—each of whom is listed in Table A-1.

I also particularly want to thank the following students for their unique and highly creative contributions: Daniel Acosta, Judy Allen, Len Ambrosini, Rafael Arredondo, Bret Bauer, Bill Blackwell, Tracy Bremmer, Paul Callanan, Carlos Caponera, Jason Chan, Jeff Chen, Yuh-Yue Chen, John Dakin, Keith Diehl, Nianbo Deng, Chad Doezie, Rich Dragon, Jason Eynon, Chuck Felder, Jim Ferguson, Francisco Galleno, Anu Grewal, Jonathan Hawkins, Gregory Herd, Sam Hoefer, Mike Hoffman, Brian Hong, Steve Houk, Allen Iftiger, Jon Iwanaga, Joseph Johnston, John Karem, Alexander Khayat, Bryan Koski, Mike Krause, Michael Laird, Joy Langley, Ben Luong, For Li, Ken Lu, Rosalind Lu, Kevin Matchett, Karen MacFarlane, Chris Metzger, Tao Mi, Kurt Myers, Mitch Needelman, Leo Nguyen, Mike Pitta, Evan Rael, David Reeves, Santiago Rydelski, Michael Saeedi, Christina Seun-Leo, Melody Shi, Martin Sobczak, Jesse Sowell, Scott Theodorson, Michael Tillman, Vu Tran, Henry Wang, Luis Vasquez, Ryan Vogel, Rose Vu, Marina Wang, Jeff Wojciechowski, Phillis Wong, Calor Yan, J. Francisco Yanez, Po Yang, Hani Yassin, Chris Yount, Rick Van Eyke, Jesus Zambrano, Er Zhang, and *especially Lisa Munro and Cecile Richardson.*

▲ **TABLE A-1** *The Master Cyclist Project All-Star Team*

Keith Abercromby	Jason Chan	Lulu Fan	Sam Hoefer
Daniel Acosta	Frank Chen	Andrew Fan	Mike Hoffman
Navid Alaghband	Yi Chia Chen	Marcello Farjalla	Andy Hollywood
Judy Allen	David Chen	Chuck Felder	Brian Hong
Carlos Amaya	Hanwen Chen	Mac Feller	Griffin Hoover
Len Ambrosini	Jeff Chen	Jim Ferguson	Griff Hoover
Birju Amin	Myron Chen	Greg Ferrell	Reza Hosseini
Andre Amiri	Yan Chen	Gary Frazier	Steve Houk
Jason Andersen	Yuh-Yue Chen	Rodney Fujiwara	Chia-Chen Hu
Dennis Ang	Michael Chiles	Alejandro Fung	Jennifer Hu
Kheng Ang	Kate Choi	Jeff Furgo	Jeffery Huang
Alberto Anon	Simon Choi	Francisco Galleno	Tony Huang
Mohammad Anwar	Shun Chow	Bill Georges	Raymond Le
Shahbaz Anwar	Julia Chu	Luis Gomez	Allen Iftiger
Rafael Arredondo	Brett Clarke	Maya Gowri	Jeff Igushi
Luke Aucoin	Jeremy Collins	W.W. Grainger	Jacqueline Interiano
Russ Barlow	Scott Cooper	Jeff Greenberg	Jon Iwanaga
Robert Barrosa	Petru Cretu	Anu Grewal	John Jerney
Ivan Batanov	John Dakin	Ann Griffith	Jerry Jew
Gregory Battersby	Charisma Davasia	George Guerrero	Hao Jiang
Bret Bauer	Anthony De La Fuente	Gerald Gutierrez	Julie Johnson
Ramin Beizaie	Nianbo Deng	Miluska Gutierrez	Joseph Johnston
Jim Bergman	Rob DePrat	Richard Haag	Craig Julien
Bill Blackwell	Sharad Deshpande	Michael Haddadin	Scott Justice
Pat Blinn	Justin Dice	Todd Halbrook	Guillermo Juvera
Geoff Bremmer	Keith Diehl	May Han	Mbugua Karanja
Tracy Bremmer	Ted Diven	Vinh Hang	John Karem
Steve Brenneman	Damon Dixon	Paul Harmeling	Chandrasekhar Karipeddi
Tim Bruce	Chad Doezie	James Harris	Arvind Kaushik
Greta Brushie	Lisa Dolan	Keith Hathaway	Go Kawasaki
Andrew Buckland	Richard Dragon	Jon Hawkins	Stephanie Ke
Phiet Bui	Ryan Dunigan	Ping He	Kevin Keegan
Gabriel Cabanas	Jason Dunn	Gregory Herd	Rohit Khanna
Paul Callanan	Feili Duosi	Robert Hermanson	Alexander Khayat
Belen Calvo	Brad Eisenstein	Zachery Hicks	Boyeon Kim
Carlos Caponera	Francine England	DeAnna Hilbrants	Ryan Kim
Peggy Carl	Kraig Enyeart	Damian Hiley	Makiko Kobayashi
Cornel Catrina	Met Ergun	Andrew Hill	Akiko Kondo
Christen Chambers	Jason Eynon	Myra Ho	

John Koontz	Chris Metzger	Haralampos Psichogios	Martin Sobczak
Bryan Koski	Kurt Meyers	Chris Purvis	Vihang Solanki
Ali Kowsari	Hitendra Mishra	Tauras Radvenis	Ryan Solomon
Michael Krause	Tao Mi	Evan Rael	Sachin Sontakke
Jason Krupoff	Avi Moghaddam	Rajiv Rajpurkar	Jesse Sowell
Dauren Kylyshpekov	Gus Monico	David Reeves	Alex Stania
Mike Laird	Richard Moreno	Indira Renduchintala	John Stedfield
Janak Lalan	Robert Motoshige	Scott Riccardella	J.P. Stocco
Maria Lam	Rashad Moumneh	Jason Richardson	Kojiro Sugiura
Brian Lane	Ali Mozayeni	Cecile Richardson	Kamran Syed
Joy Langley	Art Munda	Praveen Rikkala	Katrin Szardenings
John Lee	Lisa Munro	Jeff Root	Matt Tappan
Hosun Lee	Mark Murphy	Santiago Rydelski	Matt Tarka
Jennifer Lee	Susan Murray	Michael Saeedi	Kevin Tays
Vincenzo Lefante	Kurt Myers	Toru Sakata	Kevin Teets
Eric Li	Omar Nasir	Irina Saulea	Scott Theodorson
For Li	Sander Nauenberg	Amit Saxena	Michael Tillman
Chang W. Lleng	Dustin Neal	Dominic Schaffer	Ariel Tonnu
Jack London	Mitch Needelman	Susie Schmitt	Vu Tran
Scott Lovell	Ali Nemat	Dmitry Shmoys	Dietmar Trees
Ken Lu	Ben Newcott	Mark Searight	Kevin Trout
Rosalind Lu	Danny Nguyen	Kim Sentovich	Mitch Tsai
Gary Lu	Leo Nguyen	Max Seraj	Dennis Ulrich
Ben Luong	Yutaka Nishida	Christina Seun-Leo	Ben Uy
Anh Luu	Andrew Niu	Mihir Shah	Mike Vachani
Karen MacFarlane	Alex Norman	Hemant Sharma	Rick Van Eyke
Brendan Mahon	Jay Novak	Melody Shi	Kyri Van Hoose
Jay Mallya	Shawn O'Connell	Kane Shieh	Luis Vasquez
Kumar Mangalick	Sam Osborn	Marc Shioya	Krishna Venugopal
Donald Martens	Scott Padelsky	Brett Shipman	Apoorva Verma
Scott Martin	Archana Panukonda	Kyle Shoren	Kate Vezzetti
Kevin Matchett	Gerard Papa	Abhijeet Shrikhande	Ryan Vogel
Anu Mathur	Puneet Parashar	Napatorn Schulz	Rose Vu
Ko Matsukubo	Brady Park	Todd Sigler	Beth Walls
Josh Mauzey	Lynn Parshall	Alex Simampo	James Walsh
Naomi McAuley	Daniel Penrod	Lisa Simpson	Henry Wang
Chris McBee	Doug Petrikat	Scott Simpson	Jessica Wang
Candice McDaniel	Mike Pitta	Abhi Singh	Marina Wang
Punkaj Mehta	Michael Poirier	Vitas Sipelis	Rick Warner
Jennifer Meissen	Brennan Price	Rebecca Smith	Ilan Weinberg
Scott Merrill		Kevin Smylie	Katherine Wells

Paul Williamson

Tim Wilton

Jeff Wojciechowski

Jennifer Wold

Phillis Wong

Erin Worland

Joyce Wu

Rusen Wu

Silvia Wu

Weiya Xiao

Charles Xie

Calor Yan

J. Francisco Yanez

Jeff Yang

Po Yang

Hani Yassin

Sohmin Yee

Clinton Yip

Steve Yoon

Chris Yount

Paul Yuhas

Jesus Zambrano

David Zeng

Er Zhang

Catherine Zhou

Thanks!

A Business Cycle Primer

"Recessions teach companies to be prepared even during the good times, because a recession is like a battle—when you're in it, it's almost too late to start training for it; if you're not prepared for it, you will pay for it."

—Leonard Jaskol, former chairman and CEO,
Lydall, Inc.

I purposely avoided any technical discussion of the business cycle in the main body of this book for two reasons. First, I did not want to bore anyone already familiar with business cycle basics. Second, I did not want to bog down any nontechnical readers with unnecessary narrative weight.

In this appendix, however, I now offer a brief business cycle primer. The two main questions we want to address are as follows:

1. What exactly is the business cycle and how are its movements measured?

And, more important:

2. What are the many factors that cause the economy's movements through cycles of expansion, recession, and back to expansion?

The GDP Yardstick and Business Cycle Illustrated

Let's start, then, by defining the yardstick by which all movements in the business cycle are measured. This yardstick is the *real gross domestic product*, or GDP.

A nation's GDP measures its economic output, the *real* GDP is the GDP adjusted for inflation, and the growth in the real GDP is the way macroeconomists universally measure the overall strength or weakness of an economy.

For example, a GDP growing at an annual rate of from 2 percent to 3 percent annually reflects modest economic growth in a developed country such as the United States or Japan, whereas GDP growth in the 4 percent to 5 percent range indicates a very strong expansion. Of course, if the GDP growth rate turns negative, the economy is in recession.

It is precisely these movements of the real GDP growth rate that define the business cycle. Figure B-1 illustrates the typical progression of its roller coaster movements.

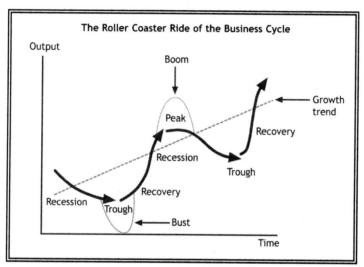

▲ **FIGURE B-1** *The roller coaster ride of the business cycle.*

Note that there is a "peak" where business activity reaches a maximum, a "trough" that is brought about by a recessionary downturn in total output, and a "recovery" or upturn in which the economy expands toward full employment. Note also that each of these phases of the cycle oscillate around a longer-term "growth trend" line.

In the figure, you can see that during some particular cycles, the economy might experience a "boom" by hitting the kind of spiked, red-hot expansionary peak shown in the figure. It might also experience a more traumatic "bust"—experiencing a severe depression rather than a more mild recession.

Of course, as you have learned in this book, during this business cycle, the fortunes of most corporations quite literally ebb and flow with the level of economic activity as corporate earnings fall and rise with the movements. Ultimately, that is why it is important to understand the business cycle.

What Business Cycles Have in Common with Fingerprints

Looking at the "regularity" of the movements in the business cycle in Figure B-1, you might jump to the very wrong conclusion that there is some "standardized" business cycle behavior in terms of how long a recession might last or even how severe it typically is. In fact, *business cycles are more like fingerprints—with no two really alike.*

This point should be evident in Table B-1, which documents how the U.S. business cycle has varied fairly dramatically since World War II in both *duration* and *amplitude.*

TABLE B-1 *The Business Cycle Since World War II*

Dates of Contraction	Duration (Months)	Maximum Negative Quarterly Growth Rate	Dates of Expansion	Duration (Months)	Maximum Positive Quarterly Growth Rate
Nov48-Oct49	11	-5.5	Oct49-July53	45	17.6
July53-May54	10	-6.3	May54-Aug57	39	11.9
Aug57-Apr58	8	-10.3	Apr58-Apr60	24	10.9
Apr60-Feb61	10	-5.0	Feb61-Dec69	106	10.3
Dec69-Nov70	11	-4.2	Nov70-Nov73	36	11.6
Nov73-Mar75	16	-5.0	Mar75-Jan80	58	16.3
Jan80-July80	6	-7.9	July80-July81	12	8.0
July81-Nov82	16	-6.5	Nov82-July90	92	9.8
July90-Mar91	8	-3.2	Mar91-Mar01	120	7.1
Mar01-Nov01	8	-1.6	-		

Sources: National Bureau of Economic Research (NBER) and Federal Reserve Board

You can see in the second column that since World War II, the shortest contraction has been a matter of just 6 months (January to July 1980), and the longest has spanned 16 months (November 1973 to March 1975 and July 1981 to November 1982). By the same token, the shortest expansion, from July 1980 to July 1981 and evident in the fifth column, has been 12 months, and the longest has been 10 *years*—the March 1991 to March 2001 "Clinton boom."

As for *amplitude* of the cycle, the third column shows that the maximum smallest quarterly negative growth rate during a contraction was –1.6. This indicates a relatively mild contraction during the March to November 2001 period. In contrast, the largest maximum quarterly negative growth was a painful –10.3 percent in the deep recession of 1957–1958.

One obvious conclusion to draw from these observations is that, as noted earlier and as with fingerprints, no two business cycles are exactly alike. *That is what makes the business cycle such a challenge to accurately forecast.*

▄▄ ▪ Why Bad Recessions Happen (Even) to Good Economies

Although every economist agrees as to what the business cycle looks like, there is much less agreement about what causes cyclical movements in general and what might trigger recessions in particular. In fact, there are three main explanations for business cycle volatility recession—each of which has its own truth, virtues, and applicability.

Explanation 1: The Shocking Horsemen of the Recessionary Apocalypse

The first explanation for business cycle volatility centers on random, external shocks to the economic system. These so-called exogenous shocks include both *negative*, recession-inducing events such as oil price spikes, increased government regulation, and war and terrorism as well as *positive*, expansion-enhancing "productivity shocks" that can result from the introduction of new technologies.

For example, as you saw in Chapter 8, "Proactive Profiting from Oil Price Spikes, Interest Rate Hikes, and Exchange Rate Risks," oil price spikes "tax" consumers on the demand side, raise production costs on the supply side, and set in motion a chain of events that can drag an economy down into the recessionary muck.

On the other hand, the positive "productivity shocks" that resulted in the 1990s from new technologies such as computers and wireless services are believed to be the single most important factor that drove the longest expansion in U.S. history—the 1990s economic boom. Likewise, deregulation in the Reagan era— which undid much of the contractionary effects of the wave of new regulations in the 1970s—is likewise believed by many economists to be a positive shock that helped facilitate the 1980s era of prosperity—albeit at some expense to the environment.

Explanation 2: Is Machiavelli (or Bozo) Guiding Fiscal and Monetary Policy

Although the exogenous shock explanation of business cycle volatility is an important one for business executives to grasp, an equally powerful second explanation is tied much more directly to the discretionary fiscal and monetary decisions of key macroeconomic policymakers—from the president and Congress on the fiscal policy side that have the power to tax and spend to the Federal Reserve and monetary policy authorities that have the ability to expand or contract both the money supply and credit.

In this explanation, the economy is typically viewed as inherently *stable*. However, it can be thrown off course by policy errors and miscalculations, or, in the worst case, by Machiavellian (or Bozo) politicians using the powers of incumbency to enhance their reelection fortunes.

For example, in the monetary policy arena, a Federal Reserve chairman might overestimate the threat of inflationary pressures because he has underestimated the rate of productivity increases and then react by orchestrating a series of interest rate hikes that turn out to be recessionary overkill. In fact, this is what many economists have accused Fed Chairman Alan Greenspan of doing in 1999 and 2000 when he tried unsuccessfully to orchestrate a "soft landing" for what he incorrectly perceived to be an overheated economy.

Similarly, in the fiscal policy arena, the president and Congress might implement unnecessary and "budget-busting" tax cuts in the months leading up to an election to—as many economists believe that President George W. Bush did prior to his 2004 reelection bid. However, in the next phase of this "political business cycle," the resultant inflation from overheating the economy and/or rising interest rates from increasing the budget deficit typically trigger a compensating "bust" after the politicians are safely in for another term.

As a final comment on the political elements of the business cycle, there is a very clear policy implication—espoused most famously by free market economists such as the monetarist Milton Friedman: The government should leave the economy alone! Of course, this advice typically goes unheeded.

Explanation 3: An Inherently Unstable System

The third major explanation of business cycle volatility relies on a much more complex and systemic view of the economy. In this view, the business cycle is driven by the "co-movements" of many variables such as income, profits, inventories, and interest rates.

From this bigger-picture perspective, a large variety of factors such as a reduction in consumer income, a falloff in corporate profits (and related inventory corrections), and/or a rise in interest rates for recessions can trigger a recession for any number of reasons. These reasons, to name just a few, include a fall in business, investor, or consumer confidence; intense spurts of speculative activity; and even instabilities in global trade flows and currency values.

To see just some of these interrelationships, consider the period leading up to the stock market collapse of March 2000. This period has been famously characterized by an infamous "irrational exuberance" and intense stock market speculation. However, when Fed Chairman Alan Greenspan chose, in his controversial words, to "prick this speculative bubble" with a series of interest rate hikes, business and investor confidence plummeted. As investors lost billions in the stock market, consumer confidence and consumption levels suffered, too. All of this helped push the economy into the March 2001 recession.

Every Explanation Is "Right"—Depending on the Recession

Of course, if you have been following this narrative closely, you might want some definitive answer on just which of the three explanations of why economies fall into recessions is the "best" one. I wish it were that simple.

In fact, depending on the particular recession, each of the explanations might be "right" to some degree. Indeed, at any given time, movements in the business cycle can be driven by very complex interactions between the various exogenous shocks, policy actions and errors, and endogenous variables in the system.

Moreover, some of the factors we have discussed, such as oil price shocks and fiscal policy errors, act like "triggers" that jolt the economy off its course. However, other factors, such as falling consumer and business confidence, might work more as "amplifiers" of any recessionary effects over a longer time frame.

The task, of course, for business executives trying to strategically manage their way through the business cycle is to understand this process in all its richness. By cultivating an awareness of the various factors that can trigger a recession as well as the role of these factors as recessionary triggers or amplifiers, "business cycle literate" executives will be better able to interpret all the data from the various economic indicators, forecasting models, and events of the macroeconomic calendar discussed in Chapter 11, "The Master Cyclist's Favorite Forecasting Tools." That is ultimately why a deeper understanding of the business cycle is so important for every would-be Master Cyclist executive.

Notes

Chapter 1

[1] Scott Berinato, "What Went Wrong at Cisco," *CIO Magazine*, August 1, 2001.

Chapter 2

[1] Aaker is the E. T. Grether Professor of Marketing and Public Policy at the Haas School of Business, U.C. Berkeley. Mascarenhas is Professor of Management at the Rutgers School of Business.

Chapter 3

[1] DRAM (dynamic random access memory) is a type of memory used in most computers, but it gets "amnesia" with any power loss. In contrast, Flash memory, which is often used in digital cameras and PDA devices such as the Palm Pilot, retains its data even after power is removed. Flash memory can also be erased and reprogrammed in blocks rather than 1 byte at a time.

Chapter 4

[1] Greer is a professor of management at the Neeley School of Business, Texas Christian University. Ireland is at the College of Business Administration, Oklahoma State University.

[2] For more details, see Michael Santoli, "Dearth of Work on Wall Street," *Barron's*, November 18, 2002.

Chapter 5

[1] The inventory turnover ratio is calculated by dividing the cost of goods sold by a firm's average inventory investment.

[2] This family of strategies also includes configure-to-order systems, which are used for products such as heavy industrial equipment and elevators and engineer-to-order where product components are specifically created to meet customers' unique requirements (for example, a specialty motor or HVAC system).

Chapter 6

[1] Shama is Anderson School of Management Foundation Professor of Management at the Robert O. Anderson School and Graduate School of Management at the University of New Mexico.

Chapter 7

[1] The fall in profits comes about when a company such as Goodyear headquartered in the United States has to take the profits it has made in Europe that are denominated in the euro currency and exchange those euros for dollars. When the dollar is strengthened relative to the euro, the euros buy fewer dollars and reduce the value of the European profits.

[2] Sarah Ellison, "In Lean Times, Big Companies Make a Grab for Market Share," *Wall Street Journal*, September 5, 2003.

Chapter 8

[1] Watkins is a member of the Economics Department at San Jose State.

[2] John Gilbert, Gen Re Capital, September 2004 Newsletter, Issue 51. www.genre.com/sharedfile/pdf/ReflectionsSept2004.pdf.

[3] There is a third kind of exchange rate risk known as *strategic risk*. When, say, the dollar strengthens against the yen, an American manufacturer such as Caterpillar will find itself at a competitive disadvantage to a Japanese competitor such as Komatsu.

[4] www.ex.ac.uk/~RDavies/arian/scandals/derivatives.html.

[5] The Nobel Laureates in question were Robert Merton and Myron Scholes, whose work on option pricing theory ironically helped create a thriving market in derivatives.

⁶ www.erisk.com/Learning/CaseStudies/ref_case_bankers.asp, Case Study, Bankers Trust, March 1, 2005.

Chapter 9

¹ *Investor's Business Daily*, Friday, April 19, 2002.

Chapter 11

¹ The Fed does have some ability to directly influence long-term rates, but its primary focus is on the short end of the yield curve.

² One of my favorite assignments for students is to have them look up the "living yield curve" at www.smartmoney.com. It shows in "movie format" how the yield curve has moved through time through its different phases.

³ Estrella is a senior vice president at the Federal Reserve Bank of New York. Mishkin is the Alfred Lerner Professor of Banking and Financial Institutions at Columbia Business School.

⁴ Bauer, Andy, Robert Eisenbeis, Daniel Waggoner, and Tao Zha, "Forecast Evaluation with Cross-Sectional Data: The Blue Chip Survey," *The Federal Reserve Bank of Atlanta*, Second Quarter 2003.

⁵ For a more complete discussion of how to use, interpret, and weigh the importance of each of these reports, you can refer to my book, *If It's Raining in Brazil, Buy Starbucks*.

⁶ The Federal Reserve granted Citigroup and Travelers a two-year trial period prior to the merger. In the interval, Congress invalidated Glass-Steagall by the passing of the Gramm-Leach-Bliley Financial Services Modernization Act of 1999.

Appendix A

[1] Eisenhardt is Professor of Strategy and Organization at Stanford University. Brown is a consultant with McKinsey & Company.

[2] If you are wondering about the title of the book, it conveys the kind of big-picture thinking I seek to foster in both investors and business executives. In this case, if rain comes to break a drought in Brazil, coffee beans will be cheaper, Starbucks will make a few cents more on its lattes, profits will rise, and so will the company's stock price. So if it rains in Brazil, buy Starbucks.

[3] For further information, see my articles: "Economics in the Cyber Classroom," *Journal of Economic Perspectives*, Spring 2000; "Policy Issues in the Teaching of Economics in Cyberspace (with Judy Shoemaker), *Contemporary Economic Policy*, July 2000; "Economics in Cyberspace: A Comparison Study" (with Judy Shoemaker), *American Journal of Distance Education*, Summer 2000; "The Power of Cyberlearning: An Empirical Test" (with Judy Shoemaker), *Journal of Computing in Higher Education*, Fall 1999.

[4] For details, see "The Hidden Potential of Macroeconomics in MBA Programs for CEO Decision Making," *Academy of Management Learning and Education*, Forthcoming, 2006.

INDEX

At **Wharton,**

We Don't **Teach**

the **Rules** of **Business...**

We Write Them.

"Great schools have... endeavored to do more than keep up to the respectable standard of a recent past; they have labored to supply the needs of an advancing and exacting world..."

— **Joseph Wharton,** *Entrepreneur and Founder of the Wharton School*

The Wharton School is recognized around the world for its innovative leadership and broad academic strengths across every major discipline and at every level of business education. It is one of four undergraduate and 12 graduate and professional schools of the University of Pennsylvania. Founded in 1881 as the nation's first collegiate business school, Wharton is dedicated to creating the highest value and impact on the practice of business and management worldwide through intellectual leadership and innovation in teaching, research, publishing and service.

Wharton's tradition of innovation includes many firsts—the first business textbooks, the first research center, the MBA in health care management—and continues to innovate with new programs, new learning approaches, and new initiatives. Today Wharton is an interconnected community of students, faculty, and alumni who are shaping global business education, practice, and policy.

Wharton is located in the center of the University of Pennsylvania (Penn) in Philadelphia, the fifth-largest city in the United States. Students and faculty enjoy some of the world's most technologically advanced academic facilities. In the midst of Penn's tree-lined, 269-acre urban campus, Wharton students have access to the full resources of an Ivy League university, including libraries, museums, galleries, athletic facilities, and performance halls. In recent years, Wharton has expanded access to its management education with the addition of Wharton West, a San Francisco academic center, and The Alliance with INSEAD in France, creating a global network.

University of Pennsylvania

www.wharton.upenn.edu

Academic Programs:

Wharton continues to pioneer innovations in education across its leading undergraduate, MBA, executive MBA, doctoral, and executive education programs.

More information about Wharton's academic programs can be found at:
http://www.wharton.upenn.edu/academics

Executive Education:

Wharton Executive Education is committed to offering programs that equip executives with the tools and skills to compete, and meet the challenges inherent in today's corporate environment. With a mix of more than 200 programs, including both open enrollment and custom offerings, a world-class faculty, and educational facilities second to none, Wharton offers leading-edge solutions to close to 10,000 executives annually, worldwide.

For more information and a complete program listing:
execed@wharton.upenn.edu (sub 4033)
215.898.1776 or 800.255.3932 ext. 4033
http://execed.wharton.upenn.edu

Research and Analysis:

Knowledge@Wharton is a unique, free resource that offers the best of business—the latest trends; the latest research on a vast range of business issues; original insights of Wharton faculty; studies, paper and analyses of hundreds of topics and industries. *Knowledge@Wharton* has over 400,000 users from more than 189 countries.

For a free subscription:
http://knowledge.wharton.upenn.edu

For licensing and content information, please contact:
Jamie Hammond,
Associate Marketing Director,
hammondj@wharton.upenn.edu • 215.898.2388

Wharton School Publishing:

Wharton School Publishing is an innovative new player in global publishing, dedicated to providing thoughtful business readers access to practical knowledge and actionable ideas that add impact and value to their professional lives. All titles are approved by a Wharton senior faculty review board to ensure they are relevant, timely, important, empirically based and/or conceptually sound, and implementable.

For author inquiries or information about corporate education and affinity programs, please contact:
Barbara Gydé, Managing Director,
gydeb@wharton.upenn.edu • 215.898.4764

The Wharton School: http://www.wharton.upenn.edu
Executive Education: http://execed.wharton.upenn.edu
Wharton School Publishing: http://whartonsp.com
Knowledge@Wharton: http://knowledge.wharton.upenn.edu

Big Winners and Big Losers
The 4 Secrets of Long-Term Business Success and Failure
BY ALFRED A. MARCUS

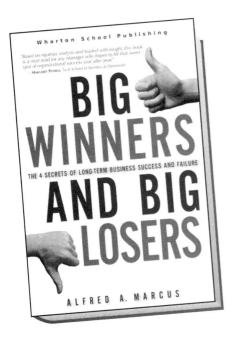

What keeps great companies winning, year after year, even as yesterday's most hyped businesses fall by the wayside? It's not what you think—or what you've read. To find the real answers, strategic management expert Alfred Marcus systematically reviewed detailed performance metrics for the 1,000 largest U.S. corporations, identifying 3% who have consistently outperformed their industry's averages for a full decade. Many of these firms get little publicity: firms like Amphenol, Ball, Family Dollar, Brown and Brown, Activision, Dreyer's, Forest Labs, and Fiserv. But their success is no accident: they've discovered patterns of success that have gone largely unnoticed elsewhere. Marcus also identified patterns associated with consistently inferior performance: patterns reflected in many of the world's most well-known companies. Drawing on this unprecedented research, *Big Winners and Big Losers* shows you what really matters most. You'll learn how consistent winners build the strategies that drive their success; how they move towards market spaces offering superior opportunity; and how they successfully manage the tensions between agility, discipline, and focus. You'll learn how to identify the right patterns of success for your company, build on the strengths you already have, realistically assess your weaknesses, and build sustainable advantage one step at a time, in a planned and logical way.

ISBN 0131451324, © 2006, 432 pp., $27.99

The Design of Things to Come
How Ordinary People Create Extraordinary Products
BY CRAIG M. VOGEL, JONATHAN CAGAN, AND PETER BOATWRIGHT

The iPod is a harbinger of a revolution in product design: innovation that targets customer emotion, self-image, and fantasy, not just product function. You'll read the hidden stories behind BodyMedia's SenseWear body monitor, Herman Miller's Mirra Chair, Swiffer's mops, OXO's potato peelers, Adidas' intelligent shoes, the new Ford F-150 pickup truck, and many other winning innovations. You'll meet the innovators, learning how they inspire and motivate their people, as they shepherd their visions through corporate bureaucracy to profitable reality. These design revolutionaries have a healthy respect for the huge cultural and economic forces swirling around them, but they've gotten past the fear of failure, in order to surf the biggest waves—and deliver the most exciting breakthroughs. Along the way, the authors deconstruct the entire process of design innovation, showing how it really works, and how today's smartest companies are innovating more effectively than ever before. *The Design of Things to Come* will fascinate you—whether you're a consumer who's intrigued by innovation or an executive who wants to deliver more of it.

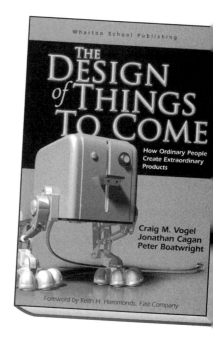

An Invitation from the Editors:
Join the
Wharton School Publishing Membership Program

Dear Thoughtful Executive,

We hope that you've discovered valuable ideas in this book, which will help you affect real change in your professional life. Each of our titles is evaluated by the Wharton School Publishing editorial board and earns the Wharton Seal of Approval — ensuring that books are timely, important, conceptually sound and/or empirically based and — key for you — implementable.

We encourage you to join the Wharton School Publishing Membership Program. Registration is simple and free, and you will receive these and other valuable benefits:

- **Access to valuable content** — receive access to additional content, including audio summaries, articles, case studies, chapters of forthcoming books, updates, and appendices.
- **Online savings** — save up to 30% on books purchased everyday at Whartonsp. com by joining the site.
- **Exclusive discounts** — receive a special discount on the Financial Times and FT.com when you join today.
- **Up to the minute information** — subscribe to select Wharton School Publishing newsletters to be the first to learn about new releases, special promotions, author appearances, and events.

Becoming a member is easy; please visit Whartonsp.com and click "Join WSP" today.

Wharton School Publishing welcomes your comments and feedback. Please let us know what interests you, so that we can refer you to an appropriate resource or develop future learning in that area. Your suggestions will help us serve you better.

Sincerely,

Jerry Wind
windj@wharton.upenn.edu

Tim Moore
tim_moore@prenhall.com

Become a member today at Whartonsp.com